CHAPTER ONE

EDITOR'S
PICKS

Boscastle

EDITOR'S PICK | FOR MORE INFO, SEE P10 |

The romantic and picturesque village of Boscastle on the north coast of Cornwall was once home to both busy fishing and stone working trades. The village sits high above the harbour and is flanked by a breath taking rugged and rocky coastline.

1

Lost Gardens of Heligan

EDITOR'S PICK | FOR MORE INFO, SEE P26 |

The Lost Gardens of Heligan is world-renowned and one of the most popular botanical gardens in England. The gardens are typical of the 19th century Gardenesque style whose design encourages gardens to be recognisable as works of art.

2

The Gurnard's Head

EDITOR'S PICK | FOR MORE INFO, SEE P32 |

A landmark pub almost at the edge of England, the Gurnard's Head is your last stop for a pint and an open fire before the Atlantic Ocean. Between St Just and Zennor, this is genuine Cornwall. Wild, mysterious and beautiful, the Gurnard's Head is an inn that transports you back to when travel was that little bit slower.

3

Eden Project

EDITOR'S PICK | FOR MORE INFO, SEE P12 |

Environmental conservation, sustainability and inspirational education are the core values of the world-renowned Eden Project. Carefully developed over many years, the geodesic domes house the world's largest indoor rainforest and a Mediterranean microclimate showcasing plants from many different habitats.

4

2 Fore Street Restaurant

EDITOR'S PICK | FOR MORE INFO, SEE P51 |

2 Fore Street is a chic Michelin-guide bistro restaurant in the little picturesque fishing village of Mousehole. This delightful find is located within the old lifeboat house. Serving all day, the courtyard and garden is a lovely spot for tea and cakes or the catch of the day.

5

Porthminster Café

EDITOR'S PICK | FOR MORE INFO, SEE P52 |

Porthminster beach is a short walk from St. Ives harbour and at this prime location is the award-winning Porthminster Café. Great for snacks, lunch or dinner, the café is renowned for its fresh and sustainable fish dishes and is a go-to place for those in the know.

6

Jamie Oliver's Fifteen

EDITOR'S PICK | FOR MORE INFO, SEE P53 |

Not much can be said about Jamie Oliver that hasn't been said already but as for the concept of Fifteen, the Cornwall branch really is something special. Oliver's first Fifteen restaurant was opened with the intention of nurturing culinary talent and training unemployed youngsters, an ethos which the Watergate Bay restaurant continues.

7

Idle Rocks

EDITOR'S PICK | FOR MORE INFO, SEE P56 |

The imposing façade of the Idle Rocks in St. Mawes dates back to 1913 and is now home to a chic, boutique hotel which boasts a fine restaurant and exceptional sea views. Dishes in the restaurant are kept simple, local and foraged wherever possible. Menus are a combination of fresh, nourishing food with a focus on sophisticated fine cuisine.

8

Alba Restaurant

EDITOR'S PICK | FOR MORE INFO, SEE P62 |

Alba is a fine dining restaurant located within a former lifeboat house behind an impressive glass facade, with exceptional sea views. Run by the classically trained chef Grant Nethercott, Alba combines techniques to create unique, modern and British cuisine.

9

Porthminster Gallery

EDITOR'S PICK | FOR MORE INFO, SEE P163 |

Porthminster Gallery is a maze of interesting exhibition rooms displaying unique and vibrant artworks. This award-winning gallery is a bright, quayside gallery for British contemporary art located in a former warehouse by the sea in St. Ives.

10

Fowey Harbour

EDITOR'S PICK | FOR MORE INFO, SEE P17 |

Fowey Harbour is nestled on the South Cornish coast between Plymouth and Falmouth. The harbour is situated on the western side of the Fowey River and bound by other towns and villages including Golant and Lostwithiel. Locals say the port is "littered with sunken boats bought by drunk amateurs".

11

The Tinner's Arms

EDITOR'S PICK | FOR MORE INFO, SEE P34 |

The Tinner's Arms is a traditional pub that is the beating heart of Zennor, and is one of Cornwall's hidden gems. This Grade II listed, 13th century pub has stone floors, low ceilings and inglenook fireplaces.

12

Museum of Witchcraft & Magic

EDITOR'S PICK | FOR MORE INFO, SEE P160 |

The Museum of Witchcraft and Magic is a museum dedicated to European witchcraft and magic and houses one of the world's largest collections of items relating to witchcraft and the occult. Since 1960, their collection has grown to more than 3,000 objects and some 7,000 books.

13

Healey's Cornish Cyder Farm

EDITOR'S PICK | FOR MORE INFO, SEE P146 |

With the focus on apples and fine flavours, Healey's newly refurbished Cornish Cyder Farm makes for a great day out for all the family. Tours run throughout the day allowing visitors to see the cider making process and take a tractor ride around the 100 acres of farm land and 20 acres of mature orchards.

14

Strong Adolfo's Café

EDITOR'S PICK | FOR MORE INFO, SEE P91 |

Strong Adolfos is how a roadside cafe should be. Located on the Atlantic Highway, this Swedish inspired eatery makes an ideal pit stop when touring this beautiful part of Cornwall. This striking building has panoramic glass windows through which you can admire the estuary at Wadebridge.

15

Genki Café

EDITOR'S PICK | FOR MORE INFO, SEE P93 |

Meaning "health and happiness" in Japanese, Genki's atmosphere, ambience and setting certainly help to nurture those benefits. This little shack close to the beach in St. Agnes provides nourishment throughout the day and you can enjoy a moment's peace and good eats in their tiered Zen garden.

16

Jubilee Pool

EDITOR'S PICK | FOR MORE INFO, SEE P25 |

This renowned art deco swimming pool in Penzance was built in 1935 and is one of the few surviving outdoor lidos from that period that remains in the UK. A welcome reminder of simple seaside Britain, the Jubilee Pool can accommodate young and old with picnic tables, a café and a covered area in case of bad weather.

17

Polperro

EDITOR'S PICK | FOR MORE INFO, SEE P20 |

One of the most popular destinations in Cornwall, Polperro is a largely unspoilt fishing village on the southeast coast. The beach here is small and sandy and sports a fabulous little tidal pool ideal for first swimmers. Pretty cottages cling to the steep hillside of this quaint and picturesque harbour.

18

The Old Quay House

EDITOR'S PICK | FOR MORE INFO, SEE P58 |

In a beautiful position on the Fowey estuary, the Old Quay House is a 19th-century riverside hotel and restaurant with a friendly and unpretentious approach to good dining. The large dining terrace is a great place for afternoon teas or sundowners with a fantastic view of the passing vessels and numerous waterfowl on the river.

19

National Maritime Museum

EDITOR'S PICK | FOR MORE INFO, SEE P161 |

Preserving Cornwall's maritime heritage is the mission of the National Maritime Museum in Falmouth, in a harbour-side location at Discovery Quay. The museum is extensive, with many excellent exhibits including an impressive collection of boats strung from the ceiling, with smaller models below.

20

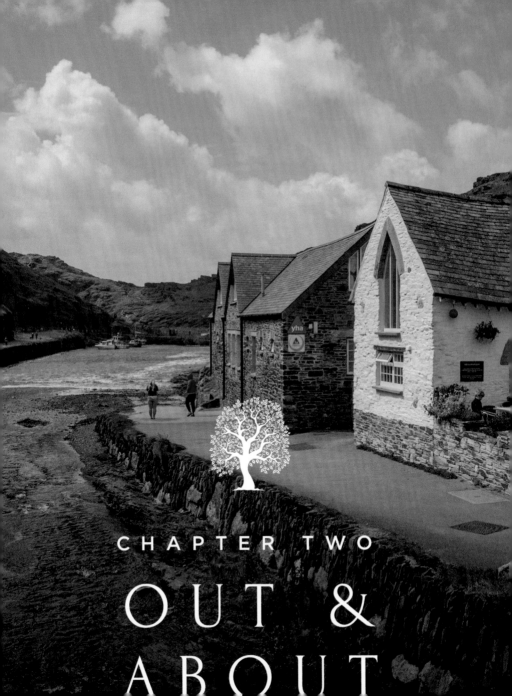

CHAPTER TWO

OUT &
ABOUT

Boscastle

OUT & ABOUT | BOSCASTLE | PL35 0HD

The romantic and picturesque village of Boscastle on the north coast of Cornwall was once home to both busy fishing and stone working trades. The village sits high above the harbour and is flanked by a breathtaking rugged and rocky coastline, perfect creative inspiration for numerous artists and writers.

In addition to the stunning natural beauty, Boscastle has a plethora of galleries, potteries, pubs and even a museum of witchcraft. An ideal base for walking and a fascinating link with times past, Boscastle is an essential stop-off for any visit to the West Country.

ADDRESS
New Road
PL35 0HD

PHONE
01840 250010

NEAR HERE
Museum of Witchcraft and Magic (p160)
Boscastle Farm Shop (p153)
The Mill House Inn (p48)

Trebarwith Strand

OUT & ABOUT | TREBARWITH | PL34 0HB

Close to Tintagel, Trebarwith Strand is a coastal settlement and popular destination for both Cornish and Devonian folk. Perfect for swimmers of all ages and complete with rock pools, cliffy outcrops and shallows, Trebarwith Strand can easily fill your day even if the weather doesn't oblige.

The Strand Café up the hill stocks beachside staples such as ice-cream and tea. If you've some experience, the surf here is good but strong. Relaxing, picturesque and often quiet, Trebarwith Strand is the ideal Cornish sunset spot, especially enjoyable with a pint from the nearby Port William pub.

ADDRESS
Trebarwith Beach
PL34 0HB

PHONE
Unavailable

NEAR HERE
The Mill House Inn (p48)

Boscastle Farm Shop (p153)

Museum of Witchcraft and

Magic (p160)

Eden Project

OUT & ABOUT | BODELVA | PL24 2SG

Environmental conservation, sustainability and inspirational education are the core values of the world-renowned Eden Project. Carefully developed over many years, the geodesic domes house the world's largest indoor rainforest and a Mediterranean microclimate showcasing plants from many different habitats.

The walks and trails of the Eden Project enable you to discover the secrets of the rainforest and experience the climate that sustains the abundant life there. The Project promotes global citizenship through community initiatives and conservation schemes. Their café is a welcome treat with fine local foods. Not to be missed.

ADDRESS

Bodelva
PL24 2SG

PHONE

01726 811911

NEAR HERE

Yummy Scrummy Bakery (p115)

Black Dog Antiques & Interiors (p131)

The Lost Gardens of Heligan (p26)

The Castle Bude

OUT & ABOUT | BUDE | EX23 8LG

A fascinating and impressive day out for the whole family, The Castle Bude includes a heritage centre, coffee shop and art gallery. Ideal for amusing the kids on those wet and windy days, The Castle Bude is a central and iconic heritage building that acts as a hub of cultural activity for this area of Cornwall.

Built by the inventor of the steam carriage, Sir Goldsworthy Gurney in 1830, The Castle embodies the spirit of Victorian engineering ingenuity and was a pioneering building in its time. The temporary galleries display contemporary art and photography while the café serves a fine cream tea overlooking the beach.

ADDRESS
The Wharf
EX23 8LG

PHONE
01288 357300

NEAR HERE
Summerleaze Beach (p27)
La Bocca Pizza Kitchen (p84)
The Beach At Bude (p81)

Readymoney Cove

OUT & ABOUT | FOWEY | PL23 1JH

Readymoney Cove is a stunning and sheltered sandy beach located to the south of the harbour town of Fowey. On a sunny day, this is a magical spot with numerous rock pools to explore and tranquil calm waters for a family swim. The imposing St Catherine's Castle sits on the opposite side of the bay.

The cove is easily accessible via a footpath and the water is safe with gentle currents. Above the beach sits the former coach house which was once the home of renowned Cornish author Daphne du Maurier. The tiny hamlet offers various rentals and dogs are allowed on the beach in the quieter months.

ADDRESS
Readymoney Road
PL23 1JH

PHONE
01726 833616

NEAR HERE
Fowey Harbour (p17)
The Webb Street Company (p138)
Quay Bakery (p156)

Looe Harbour

OUT & ABOUT | LOOE | PL13 1DX

Looe is one of the most picturesque fishing villages in Cornwall and has a bustling fishing port with fishermen bringing in their catches daily. The distinctive houses here traditionally had their living areas upstairs due to the very common floods in the town.

Boat excursions run to nearby Looe Island, a nature reserve which makes an excellent family day out. The steep-sided valley of the river Looe is the site of evidence of habitation going back to prehistoric times. Over the years Looe grew to become a major port by the 1400s.

ADDRESS

The Quay
PL13 1DX

PHONE

01503 262839

NEAR HERE

The Old Sail Loft (p85)

Trawlers on the Quay (p78)

The Blue Peter Inn (p36)

Portscatho

OUT & ABOUT | PORTSCATHO | TR2 5HH

Situated on the Roselands peninsula near to Truro on the edge of Gerrans Bay, Portscatho is a delightful part of Cornwall and a great area for walks around the harbour, the coastal path and the nearby beach. The steep slope down to the beach means that the views from the village itself are exceptional in all directions.

Portscatho is popular with foodies and is known for its outstanding food shops, restaurants and pubs. Portscatho is a great destination to spend an afternoon nurturing a pint of Cornish ale, a cream tea or a traditional pasty. The village also hosts a vibrant fish festival in August.

ADDRESS
The Lugger
TR2 5HH

PHONE
Unavailable

NEAR HERE
The Harbour Gallery (p170)
Tatams (p114)
The Watch House (p79)

Fowey Harbour

OUT & ABOUT | FOWEY | PL23 1AJ

Fowey Harbour is nestled on the South Cornish coast between Plymouth and Falmouth. The harbour is situated on the western side of the Fowey River and bound by other towns and villages including Golant and Lostwithiel. Locals say the port is "littered with sunken boats bought by drunk amateurs".

The large natural harbour has always been an important maritime access point and is part of the southern Cornish area of Outstanding Natural Beauty. Fishing, sailing and other water sports are all popular here and the harbour and its surrounds are great places to explore by foot, car or boat.

ADDRESS

Albert Quay
PL23 1AJ

PHONE

01726 832471

NEAR HERE

The Old Quay House (p58)

Quay Bakery (p156)

The Webb Street Company (p138)

Polperro

OUT & ABOUT | POLPERRO | PL13

One of the most popular destinations in Cornwall, Polperro is a largely unspoilt fishing village on the southeast coast. The beach here is small and sandy and sports a fabulous little tidal pool ideal for first swimmers. Pretty cottages cling to the steep hillside of this quaint and picturesque harbour.

Free from traffic, Polperro is equally enjoyable for browsing, wandering and eating with its many independent shops, noteworthy seafood restaurants and galleries. The relaxed town is also a great starting point for cliff walks in both directions with fantastic views.

ADDRESS
Quay Road
PL13

PHONE
Unavailable

NEAR HERE
The Three Pilchards (p40)
The Blue Peter Inn (p36)
The Old Sail Loft (p85)

Bude Sea Pool

OUT & ABOUT | **BUDE** | EX23 8HN

Created in the 1930s to provide safe and comfortable swimming, Bude Sea Pool is a great community facility and totally free of charge. The semi-natural pool was created under the curve of the cliff and provides a lovely spot to swim sheltered from the often extreme Atlantic Ocean.

Now administered by the independent Friends of Bude Sea Pool Charity, it is a focal point on the Bude section of the coast. At 88 metres long and 43 metres wide, the pool makes a great place for a workout. The facilities are constantly improving and the care and devotion of the charity mean it is well worth supporting.

ADDRESS
Sea Pool
EX23 8HN

PHONE
01288 354240

NEAR HERE
Summerleaze Beach (p27)
The Castle Bude (p13)
La Bocca Pizza Kitchen (p84)

Port Isaac

OUT & ABOUT | PORT ISAAC | PL29

The word picturesque could have been coined for Port Isaac. The narrow winding streets are lined with whitewashed cottages, many of which are now listed due to their historical importance and pleasing aesthetic. Wander down to the harbour where you will find local fishermen landing their daily catch each morning.

Port Isaac is set amidst rugged and magnificent scenery on Cornwall's North coast from where you can begin stunning coastal walks, visit Polzeath Beach or head out on a boat trip. Port Isaac has become a popular stop off with fans of the TV series Doc Martin starring Martin Clunes which is filmed here.

ADDRESS
Fore Street
PL29

PHONE
Unavailable

NEAR HERE
The Golden Lion (p41)
Outlaw's Fish Kitchen (p76)
Kiln (p134)

Rock Beach

OUT & ABOUT | ROCK | PL27 6LD

On the eastern shore of the Camel Estuary, the village of Rock has a reputation as an upmarket holiday destination for the yachting set. The beach is a long stretch of golden sand which follows the estuary to the coast. The sand dunes behind mask the renowned and prestigious St Enodoc golf course.

The beach is spacious enough for a spot to be found even in the height of summer, while the local area of Outstanding Natural Beauty is known for its waterfowl. Set opposite Padstow, Rock has been referred to as "Kensington on Sea" but actually all are welcome and it's a great beach.

ADDRESS
Rock Road
PL27 6LD

PHONE
Unavailable

NEAR HERE
Blue Tomato (p111)

Rick Stein, The Seafood Restaurant (p71)

St Petroc's Bistro (p65)

Fistral Beach

OUT & ABOUT | NEWQUAY | TR7 1HY

One of the world's top surfing destinations, eager surfers flock to Fistral for the big waves and surf scene. Many of the UK's biggest surf competitions take place here and whether you are a pro or a beginner, Fistral is ideal as the two headlands funnel in the big waves while providing more manageable surf between.

Bodhi's Beach Cafe offers a range of drinks and snacks throughout the main holiday seasons and the imposing grandeur of the Headland Hotel looks out over the beach. On shore there are plenty of opportunities to book surf lessons or hire gear and a number of takeaways including Rick Stein's popular fish and chip shop.

ADDRESS

Headland Road
TR7 1HY

PHONE

01637 838516

NEAR HERE

Rick Stein, Fistral (p66)

The Harbour Fish & Grill (p70)

The Boathouse (p89)

Jubilee Pool

OUT & ABOUT | PENZANCE | TR18 4FF

This renowned art deco swimming pool in Penzance was built in 1935 and is one of the few surviving outdoor lidos from that period that remains in the UK. A welcome reminder of simple seaside Britain, the Jubilee Pool can accommodate young and old with picnic tables, a café and a covered area in case of bad weather.

The pool sports an unusual triangular yet curved design which nestles close to the sea while being protected by high walls. With classes and other activities regularly held, the Jubilee Pool is a charming and satisfying place to spend a day relaxing in the delightful Art Deco surroundings.

ADDRESS
Battery Road
TR18 4FF

PHONE
01736 369224

NEAR HERE
The Cornish Barn (p64)
No.56 (p73)
The Honey Pot (p100)

The Lost Gardens of Heligan

OUT & ABOUT | ST. AUSTELL | PL26 6EN

The Lost Gardens of Heligan is world-renowned and one of the most popular botanical gardens in England. The gardens are typical of the 19th century Gardenesque style whose design encourages gardens to be recognisable as works of art.

Unveiled in 1992 from under decades of overgrowth, the 200 acres of the Lost Gardens were rediscovered having been devoured by the brambles. The Heligan Tearoom provides Cornish cream teas and home-cooked lunches, incorporating fresh seasonal produce from the gardens and estate. Well behaved dogs are welcome if kept on a lead.

ADDRESS

Pentewan
PL26 6EN

PHONE

01726 845100

NEAR HERE

Lobbs Farm Shop (p150)

The Sharksfin (p46)

The Kings Arms (p35)

Summerleaze Beach

OUT & ABOUT | BUDE | EX23 8HN

Within easy walking distance of Bude, Summerleaze Beach never feels too crowded due to the huge expanse of golden sands. The unusual large breakwater protects the small harbour and the mouth of the Bude canal, with its bobbing fishing boats.

Given the location and the surf break, the beach is particularly popular with families and surfers. Not just a flat expanse, Summerleaze Beach has rock pools around the edges and is great for walking and dogs can be taken in the low season. A sea-water bathing pool on the opposite side of the beach makes for safe bathing in all conditions.

ADDRESS

Summerleaze Crescent
EX23 8HN

PHONE

01288 354240

NEAR HERE

Bude Sea Pool (p21)

The Castle Bude (p13)

La Bocca Pizza Kitchen (p84)

Mevagissey

OUT & ABOUT | ST. AUSTELL | PL26 6UQ

Mevagissey is an attractive village and fishing port five miles south of St. Austell. This was once the centre of Cornwall's pilchard fishery with boat building traditions dating back to 1745. The village still boasts a working harbour with local fisherman heading out each morning.

The name Mevagissey is derived from the names of two saints, St Meva and St Issey and dates back to 1313. From the top of Polkirt Hill there is a great view over the cobbled streets, the harbour and the yachting pool. Mevagissey is also ideally located for a visit to the nearby Lost Gardens of Heligan.

ADDRESS

The Harbour
PL26 6UQ

PHONE

Unavailable

NEAR HERE

The Sharksfin (p46)

The Kings Arms (p35)

The Lost Gardens of Heligan (p26)

CHAPTER THREE

PUBLIC
HOUSES

The Gurnard's Head

PUBLIC HOUSES | ST. IVES | TR26 3DE

A landmark pub almost at the edge of England, the Gurnard's Head is your last stop for a pint and an open fire before the Atlantic Ocean. Between St Just and Zennor, this is genuine Cornwall. Wild, mysterious and beautiful, the Gurnard's Head is an inn that transports you back to when travel was that little bit slower.

With excellent dining and rooms with comfortable beds, the Gurnard's Head is both a welcome stop-off and a destination in itself. The food is simple, fresh, local wherever possible and of exceptional quality. As such, this pub regularly features in national pub guides and has a loyal following.

ADDRESS

Nr Zennor
TR26 3DE

PHONE

01736 796928

NEAR HERE

The Tinner's Arms (p34)

Halsetown Inn (p45)

Scoff Troff Cafe (p108)

Beerwolf Books

PUBLIC HOUSES | FALMOUTH | TR11 3AZ

No wolf to speak of but this tucked away Falmouth pub certainly has a fine selection of beer and a well-stocked bookshop. A winning combination for drinkers and readers of all persuasions, this freehouse has a great atmosphere and welcomes locals and visitors alike.

The pub was voted as the coolest pub in Britain by the Times in 2017 who said "A wonderful space in the former home of the Falmouth Working Men's Club, this is a reinvention of the whole idea of the pub, with two threatened urban institutions coming together to create something that feels surprisingly vital."

ADDRESS

3 Bells Court
TR11 3AZ

PHONE

01326 618474

NEAR HERE

Courtyard Deli & Kitchen (p109)

Baker Tom's (p118)

Falmouth Art Gallery (p166)

The Tinner's Arms

PUBLIC HOUSES | ST. IVES | TR26 3BY

The Tinner's Arms is a traditional pub that is the beating heart of Zennor, and is one of Cornwall's hidden gems. This Grade II listed, 13th century pub has stone floors, low ceilings and inglenook fireplaces.

At the centre of the village for over 700 years, the pub has provided welcoming refuge, a roaring fire and a fine pint of ale ever since. First built for the masons working on the church of Saint Senara in the village, this is still the only pub in town, and as in the past, the food is hearty, satisfying and locally sourced.

ADDRESS

Zennor
TR26 3BY

PHONE

01736 796927

NEAR HERE

The Gurnard's Head (p32)

Halsetown Inn (p45)

Porthminster Beach Cafe (p52)

The Kings Arms

PUBLIC HOUSES | MEVAGISSEY | PL26 6UQ

This small traditional inn is a charming, pared back pub in the harbour town of Mevagissey. The owners Kris and Helen are passionate about serving good quality food at reasonable prices. They describe their food as "ad hoc" and their small but perfectly selected menu reflects the changing of the seasons. Daily specials are decided based on what turns up on the dock that day.

They like to keep busy and also run Meva Wines, Meva Bakery and The Barrel & Mackerel Food School from the pub to promote local produce and great cooking as best they can.

ADDRESS

17 Fore Street
PL26 6UQ

PHONE

01726 843904

NEAR HERE

The Kings Arms (p35)

The Sharksfin (p46)

The Lost Gardens of Heligan
(p26)

The Blue Peter Inn

PUBLIC HOUSES | POLPERRO | PL13 2QZ

Sitting on the harbour wall of the stunning village of Polperro, the Blue Peter Inn offers a warm welcome to all comers. They offer great beer, food, superb views and live music for which its fame has spread far and wide. They do their best to ensure the journey from the sea to your plate is a short one which isn't difficult given their location.

Supporting and developing the local music scene is an important part of what the Blue Peter Inn stands for, which makes this a vibrant venue to spend an evening. As a free house the Blue Peter offers an eclectic mix of real ales, ciders and lagers along with mulled wine in the winter months.

ADDRESS

Quay Road
PL13 2QZ

PHONE

01503 272743

NEAR HERE

Polperro (p20)

The Three Pilchards (p40)

The Old Sail Loft (p85)

The Chintz Symposium

PUBLIC HOUSES | FALMOUTH | TR11 2BY

You'll see why the name fits after your first visit to the Chintz Symposium. The eclectic and bohemian decor is paired with the rustic original wooden beams and floors. Not your run-of-the-mill wine bar, the Chintz Symposium mixes fantasy and creativity for a trip down the rabbit-hole to meet Alice on the other side.

Red velvet chairs, ornate gold furniture a mini library, tapestry rugs and a chandelier all combine in a wondrous and creative atmosphere. If you are a fan of the pared down, minimalist shades of grey look then this perhaps isn't the place for you.

ADDRESS
Old Brewery Yard
TR11 2BY

PHONE
01326 617550

NEAR HERE
Toro Studio (p122)
Stones Bakery (p157)
Star & Garter (p47)

The Three Pilchards

PUBLIC HOUSES | POLPERRO | PL13 2QZ

The oldest pub in Polperro, the Three Pilchards is situated on the quay where fish have been landed by local fisherman for centuries. Being steeped in charm and history, this family friendly pub is popular with locals and visitors alike.

With stories of smugglers and intrigue abounding, the Three Pilchards is a pub with more than just pints of ale and cosy log fires to tempt you in. It's a great place to base yourself and head off to walk the cliffs or from which to head out on a boat ride.

ADDRESS

Quay Road
PL13 2QZ

PHONE

01503 272233

NEAR HERE

The Blue Peter Inn (p36)

Polperro (p20)

The Old Sail Loft (p85)

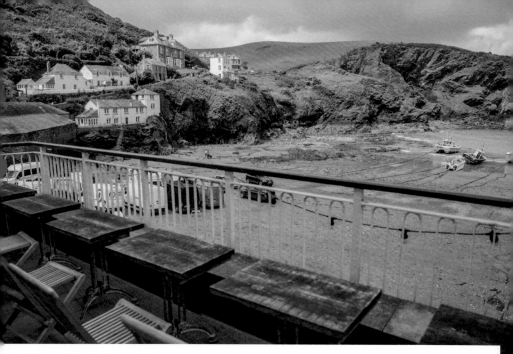

The Golden Lion

PUBLIC HOUSES | PORT ISAAC | PL29 3RB

This 18th-century pub in Port Isaac is awash with charm and history. Overlooking the stunning bay makes this an ideal spot to watch the beautiful blues of summer calm and the dramatic greys of winter storms. The Golden Lion takes pride in their cask ale and serves a fine fish and chips.

The cosy old-world dining room upstairs perfectly complements the informal bar below and if weather permits you can drink in the views from the terrace outside. The Golden Lion also houses the infamous "bloody bones bar" that sports a secret tunnel for sneaking booty in and out.

ADDRESS

10 Fore Street
PL29 3RB

PHONE

01208 880336

NEAR HERE

Outlaw's Fish Kitchen (p76)

Kiln (p134)

Port Gaverne Restaurant (p80)

The Ship Inn

PUBLIC HOUSES | WADEBRIDGE | PL27 6DF

One of the oldest Inns in Wadebridge, the award-winning, 16th century Ship Inn has recently been refurbished and now boasts a fresh, modern look. The historic features have been retained including nautical memorabilia, open fires and beautiful exposed stone.

This is a straightforward Cornish pub and a fine one at that. The focus is on community and, as such, is a hit with the locals. The menu consists of simple pub grub made with local ingredients which is updated daily. Try the catch of the day from nearby Newlyn fish market.

ADDRESS

Gonvena Hill
PL27 6DF

PHONE

01208 813845

NEAR HERE

Goose Shed (p120)

Strong Adolfos Cafe (p91)

The Arc Food Store (p141)

The Miners Arms

PUBLIC HOUSES | ST. AGNES | TR5 0QF

The Miners Arms has been serving the locals in Mithian near St. Agnes since the 16th century. This quaint pub has a rich history and throughout its life and has been a courthouse, a venue for inquests and even a smugglers' lair. Ghosts of smugglers past have been known to return to finish their drinks and settle scores from time to time.

This old-school Cornish pub offers delicious traditional meals including a great Sunday roast and classic pub pies. It is off the beaten track but well worth the detour for a warm welcome and an authentic Cornish experience.

ADDRESS
Mithian
TR5 0QF

PHONE
01872 552375

NEAR HERE
Genki Café (p93)
Q Tearoom, Studio (p105)
Healey's Cyder Farm (p146)

Ship Inn

PUBLIC HOUSES | MOUSEHOLE | TR19 6QX

Full of Cornish character and charm, the Ship Inn in Mousehole is a friendly pub with eight comfortable rooms offering splendid views of the sea and quaint Mousehole harbour. The bar and restaurant serve fresh local food all year round and the traditional Cornish pub food is accompanied by the excellent St. Austell ales.

The pub's position gives them great access to some of the finest fish in the British Isles and their home cooking truly has the taste of Cornwall in every dish. Low ceilings, wooden beams and open fires add to the cosy character.

ADDRESS

South Cliff
TR19 6QX

PHONE

01736 731234

NEAR HERE

2 Fore Street Restaurant (p51)
Sandpiper Gallery (p171)

Halsetown Inn

PUBLIC HOUSES | ST. IVES | TR26 3NA

The Halsetown Inn is a cosy, quirky and traditional pub with an eco-ethos offering real ales and Cornish cream teas. The pub is a short drive from St. Ives and off the beaten track but is a hidden gem that dates back to 1832.

The menu is of the gastro ilk with dishes including pan fried scallops with chilli jam, ham hock terrine and slow roasted pork belly. Ideal when washed down with a bottle of local sparkler, Camel Valley or a tea from nearby Tregothnan, the UK's only tea estate.

ADDRESS
Halsetown
TR26 3NA

PHONE
01736 795583

NEAR HERE
Porthminster Beach Cafe (p52)
Scoff Troff Cafe (p108)
Harbour Fish & Chips (p59)

The Sharksfin

PUBLIC HOUSES | MEVAGISSEY | PL26 6QU

The Sharksfin is an excellent place to stop for a drink and quick bite to eat before exploring this picturesque and historic harbour. A traditional yet stylish bar and restaurant, the Sharksfin is decked out with a vibrant interior and has a menu with an American twist.

Located directly on the harbour side of this bustling fishing port, the Sharksfin provides a fascinating window seat from which to observe real Cornish life. Combined with chargrilled local sardines or a juicy steak, we think makes this a winning combination.

ADDRESS
The Quay
PL26 6QU

PHONE
01726 842969

NEAR HERE
Mevagissey (p30)

The Kings Arms (p35)

Lost Gardens of Heligan (p26)

Star & Garter

PUBLIC HOUSES | FALMOUTH | TR11 2AF

The Star and Garter is a 19th-century pub with a distinctly contemporary menu. It can't be beaten for its views over Falmouth harbour from where they receive most of their fish. The meat served at the Star is also cured and smoked on the premises.

The highlight of the week is the Sunday roast but the combined talents of the chefs always produce something special every day of the week. The Star isn't just about food - its long list of whiskeys and rums are matched by sprightly and creative cocktails. They also have two apartments which continue the heritage nautical theme of the pub.

ADDRESS

52 High Street
TR11 2AF

PHONE

01326 316663

NEAR HERE

Toro Studio (p122)

The Chintz Symposium (p37)

Courtyard Deli & Kitchen (p109)

The Mill House Inn

PUBLIC HOUSES | TINTAGEL | PL34 0HD

Set above the lovely Trebarwith Strand, the Mill House is located between the picturesque Boscastle and the fascinating Port Isaac. The former corn mill nestles in its own seven-acre wooded valley and offers accommodation in addition to well kept ales and fine food.

The rooms are comfortable, well sized and of a high standard while the food is generous and reasonably priced. Sunday lunches here are a particular favourite. The scenic beauty of the area makes the Mill House a great spot for a walking break or an overnight stay for exploring the dramatic coastline.

ADDRESS

Trebarwith Strand
PL34 0HD

PHONE

01840 770200

NEAR HERE

The Mill House Inn (p48)

Boscastle Farm Shop (p153)

Museum of Witchcraft & Magic (p160)

Old Custom House

PUBLIC HOUSES | PADSTOW | PL28 8BL

Nestled within the harbour town of Padstow is the Old Custom House, a B&B and restaurant known for its excellent quality and service. There is a stylish and intimate bar along with comfortable guest rooms and a well-equipped spa. The Old Custom House directly overlooks the bustling harbour and sits in the midst of the hustle and bustle of this attractive harbour.

Food and drinks range from freshly brewed fair trade coffee and local ales, to fresh Cornish shellfish. The Old Custom House strives to provide the best local food served in a home-cooked way and will rarely disappoint.

ADDRESS

South Quay
PL28 8BL

PHONE

01841 532359

NEAR HERE

St Petroc's Bistro (p65)

Burgers & Fish (p63)

The Seafood Restaurant (p71)

CHAPTER FOUR

PLACES TO EAT

2 Fore Street Restaurant

PLACES TO EAT | MOUSEHOLE | TR19 6QU

2 Fore Street is a chic Michelin-guide bistro restaurant in the little picturesque fishing village of Mousehole. This delightful find is located within the old lifeboat house. Serving all day, the courtyard and garden is a lovely spot for tea and cakes or the catch of the day.

Owned by Joe Wardell, who trained under Raymond Blanc, expect shell-roasted scallops with lemon and basil butter, sea bass with puy lentils and roast tomatoes or crab florentine. This harbour side restaurant is also blessed with one of the finest views in town. Ask for a table by the window and watch Mousehole life go by.

ADDRESS

2 Fore Street
TR19 6QU

PHONE

01736 731164

NEAR HERE

Ship Inn (p44)

The Mousehole (p129)

Porthminster Beach Café

PLACES TO EAT | ST. IVES | TR26 2EB

Porthminster beach is a short walk from St. Ives harbour and at this prime location is the award-winning Porthminster Café. Great for snacks, lunch or dinner, the café is renowned for its fresh and sustainable fish dishes and is a go-to place for those in the know.

One of the cleanest beaches in the South West, Porthminster is a great escape from the crowded streets of St. Ives. The café is housed under the cliff at Porthminster Point in an elegant Art Deco building with high ceilings and jaunty decor. There are few more enjoyable places to spend an afternoon than one sat in the sunshine on the terrace of this café.

ADDRESS

Porthminster Beach,
Carbis Bay
TR26 2EB

PHONE

01736 795352

NEAR HERE

Porthminster Gallery (p163)

Armstrong & Wing (p133)

Scoff Troff Cafe (p108)

Jamie Oliver's Fifteen

PLACES TO EAT | WATERGATE BAY | TR8 4AA

Not much can be said about Jamie Oliver that hasn't been said already but as for the concept of Fifteen, the Cornwall branch really is something special. Oliver's first Fifteen restaurant was opened with the intention of nurturing culinary talent and training unemployed youngsters, an ethos which the Watergate Bay restaurant continues.

The restaurant provides seasonal food served with originality and creativity. A great place for a special treat or just to experience the fabulous views of Watergate Bay. All profits generated by the restaurant go to the Cornwall Food Foundation - the restaurant's registered charity.

ADDRESS

Watergate Road
TR8 4AA

PHONE

01637 861000

NEAR HERE

Catch Seafood, Bar & Grill (p67)

Town & Country Kitchen (p113)

The Boathouse (p89)

Idle Rocks

PLACES TO EAT | ST. MAWES | TR2 5AN

The imposing façade of the Idle Rocks in St. Mawes dates back to 1913 and is now home to a chic, boutique hotel which boasts a fine restaurant and exceptional sea views. Dishes in the restaurant are kept simple, local and foraged wherever possible. Menus are a combination of fresh, nourishing food with a focus on sophisticated fine cuisine.

The current incarnation of one of St. Mawes' most striking edifices is a relaxed and lively venue with a large terrace to sit and enjoy the sun. Family friendly too.

ADDRESS
Tredenham Road
TR2 5AN

PHONE
01326 270270

NEAR HERE
The Watch House (p79)
The Harbour Gallery (p170)
Tatams (p114)

Mackerel Sky Seafood Bar

PLACES TO EAT | NEWLYN | TR18 5PZ

In the heart of the fishing village of Newlyn lives a charming little restaurant on a humpbacked bridge, passionate about the fresh fish served there. The restaurant is a great place for the indecisive seafood lover- all the dishes are "taster size" so you can combine your mackerel burger with a scallop, some fresh crab or a simple bowl of chips.

The lovely decor of the little bar and the friendly staff make this a very relaxed and pleasurable stop off whether for a full-on meal or a quick snack. Well worth seeking out but closed through the autumn and winter months.

ADDRESS

New Road
TR18 5PZ

PHONE

01736 448982

NEAR HERE

The Honey Pot (p100)

Trelawney Fish & Deli (p155)

Stevenson Newlyn (p143)

The Old Quay House

PLACES TO EAT | FOWEY | PL23 1AQ

In a beautiful position on the Fowey estuary, the Old Quay House is a 19th-century riverside hotel and restaurant with a friendly and unpretentious approach to good dining. The large dining terrace is a great place for afternoon teas or sundowners with a fantastic view of the passing vessels and numerous waterfowl on the river.

Once a refuge for sailors, the Old Quay House is now a luxury boutique hotel with exclusive and tasteful rooms offering chic sophistication by the sea. Ideal for exploring this charming town, the Old Quay House is an elegant and satisfying choice.

ADDRESS

28 Fore Street
PL23 1AQ

PHONE

01726 833302

NEAR HERE

Havener's (p87)

The Webb Street Company
(p138)

Fowey Harbour (p17)

Harbour Fish & Chips

PLACES TO EAT | ST. IVES | TR26 1LF

Simple and fresh ingredients meet a sleek and bright interior at Harbour Fish & Chips. This stylish and simple restaurant is located on The Wharf Harbour in St. Ives and provides excellent views of the water front. The menu is focused on traditional Fish & Chips using fresh quality ingredients that are brought in daily by local fishermen.

Choose from battered or grilled for a healthier option. When available, local shellfish are featured including fresh mussels and scallops. This is a fish and chip experience a cut above the usual.

ADDRESS

4 Wharf Road
TR26 1LF

PHONE

01736 799295

NEAR HERE

Alba Restaurant (p62)

Hub (p75)

Scoff Troff Cafe (p108)

The Balcony Bar & Kitchen

PLACES TO EAT | ST. IVES | TR26 1LP

The Balcony Bar & Kitchen is a relaxed restaurant located on the harbour front which makes it a great place to watch the world of St. Ives go by while enjoying a chilled glass of Cornish cider. Surfboards line the ceiling along with vibrant coloured graphics and road signs that give it a 60s American diner feel.

Perfect for a classic full english breakfast or french toast and lovely for lunch with crowd pleasers such as halloumi burgers and spicy nachos. Not ideal if you are looking to loose a few pounds or after a quiet spot for a chat.

ADDRESS

The Wharf
TR26 1LP

PHONE

01736 798482

NEAR HERE

Hub (p75)

Harbour Fish & Chips (p59)

57 Fore Street (p73)

Hubbox

PLACES TO EAT | TRURO | TR1 3DJ

After outgrowing their original location, Hubbox is currently located inside a beautiful 19th-century Grade II listed Wesleyan chapel. The interior is a stylish contrast to the historic surroundings and is matched by the modern menu and hand-picked craft beers.

Hubbox takes inspiration from American street food with dishes including crispy buttermilk chicken, slow-smoked beef brisket and slow cooked pulled pork. The Executive Chef Alex Towill worked in New York and has brought a taste of the Big Apple to the heart of Truro, one of a growing number of these outlets in the South West.

ADDRESS

116 Kenwyn Street
TR1 3DJ

PHONE

01872 240700

NEAR HERE

Truro Cathedral (p169)

Grounded (p103)

Falmouth Bay Seafood Café (p88)

Alba Restaurant

PLACES TO EAT | ST. IVES | TR26 1LP

Alba is a fine dining restaurant located within a former lifeboat house behind an impressive glass facade, with exceptional sea views. Run by the classically trained chef Grant Nethercott, Alba combines techniques to create unique, modern and British cuisine.

Expect St Bay mackerel niçoise, ham hock and foie gras terrine and Cornish fish soup. St. Ives is certainly not short of great restaurants but Alba stands out from the rest. Booking is recommended as it is very popular.

ADDRESS

Wharf Road
TR26 1LP

PHONE

01736 797222

NEAR HERE

Harbour Fish & Chips (p59)

Hub (p75)

The Balcony Bar & Kitchen (p60)

Burgers & Fish

PLACES TO EAT | PADSTOW | PL28 8AJ

This unique and bustling Padstow eatery is an excellent pit stop after a busy day exploring the coastal landscape. Burgers & Fish is a simple concept, a friendly relaxed restaurant that serves delicious gourmet charcoal grilled burgers. The restaurant is a few steps from the harbour front and run by the former head chef of Nathan Outlaw's restaurant who combines fish and meat with flair.

All of their dishes are chargrilled on an open fire and their pickles and preserves are home made. The friendly atmosphere and spacious leather booths serve to create a dining experience that rivals any of the many other Padstow food stops.

ADDRESS

1A The Strand
PL28 8AJ

PHONE

01841 532884

NEAR HERE

St Petroc's Bistro (p65)
Old Custom House (p49)
The Seafood Restaurant (p71)

The Cornish Barn

PLACES TO EAT | PENZANCE | TR18 4AW

Seek out the fun and lively atmosphere of the Cornish Barn, a smokehouse in Penzance's quiet backstreets. The spacious interior, terrace and beer garden provide comfortable surroundings for a hearty breakfast, lunchtime burgers and evening mains of home-smoked, locally sourced meats and fish.

A breath of fresh air in Penzance, the Cornish Barn has a contemporary and trendy feel, welcoming regular locals and tourists alike. Its reputation is spreading and it's definitely worth a visit if you are looking for a change from the more standard Cornish pub grub.

ADDRESS
20 Chapel Street
TR18 4AW

PHONE
01736 339414

NEAR HERE
No.56 (p73)
The Honey Pot (p100)
Ian Lentern Butchers (p147)

St. Petroc's Bistro

PLACES TO EAT | PADSTOW | PL28 8EA

An airy hotel and restaurant situated in picturesque Padstow, St. Petroc's Bistro is one of many restaurants and enterprises owned by celebrity chef Rick Stein. The bistro is situated within an attractive, rustic building with low wooden beams, winding stairs and cosy fireplaces.

The décor of this modest bistro is elegant and informal with the blue velvet parlour chairs and vibrant paintings. Enjoy drinks in their cosy snug bar, the relaxed lounge or dine in the pretty garden courtyard. The signature Stein simplicity is reflected in the seafood starters and the perfectly done grilled dishes.

ADDRESS

4 New Street
PL28 8EA

PHONE

01841 532700

NEAR HERE

The Seafood Restaurant (p71)

Old Custom House (p49)

Burgers & Fish (p63)

Rick Stein, Fistral

PLACES TO EAT | NEWQUAY | TR7 1HY

The wonderfully relaxed atmosphere of Fistral Beach in Newquay is echoed in Rick Stein's restaurant. Friendly and laid-back, Fistral is a great place to enjoy a quick fish burger during lunch on the beach or Indian and Thai-inspired cuisine at night.

The interior is open plan with wall to wall windows overlooking the beach, making for a perfect backdrop to grab a bench and enjoy cod, haddock or lemon sole with a warm bag of chips and a cold glass of beer. Home-made sauces such as tartare and curry make fine accompaniments to any meal and Stein's mark of quality shines through.

ADDRESS
Headland Road
TR7 1HY

PHONE
01637 303103

NEAR HERE
Fistral Beach (p24)
The Harbour Fish & Grill (p70)
The Boathouse (p89)

Catch Seafood, Bar & Grill

PLACES TO EAT | MAWGAN PORTH | TR8 4BA

A stylish bar and grill located in Mawgan Porth, just steps away from the stunning beach and sandwiched between two stunning Cornish cliffs. Catch creates dishes and tapas to share along with fresh fish, pasta and burgers. Favourites include fruits de la mer and fresh lobster salad.

The interior is elegant, simple and bright, while service is laid back and friendly. The large deck makes a lovely setting to watch the sun go down if the weather allows. Open all day, every day.

ADDRESS

Mawgan Porth Beach
TR8 4BA

PHONE

01637 860372

NEAR HERE

Jamie Oliver's Fifteen (p53)

Town & Country Kitchen (p113)

Strong Adolfos Cafe (p91)

The Harbour Fish & Grill

PLACES TO EAT | NEWQUAY | TR7 1HF

In a prime location built into the cliff and overlooking seven of Newquay's finest beaches is the Harbour Fish and Grill. A relaxed, al fresco style restaurant with a stylish interior and a sun drenched terrace. From breakfast to a sumptuous tasting menu to creative fish main courses, the choice could leave you reeling but there's little to disappoint.

Converted from a grain store in the 1930s it became a hotel and restaurant in the 1950s. Now, this lovely period building makes a charming cliff top getaway from which to watch the hubbub of Newquay.

ADDRESS
North Quay Hill
TR7 1HF

PHONE
01637 873040

NEAR HERE
The Boathouse (p89)
Rick Stein, Fistral (p66)
Fistral Beach (p24)

Rick Stein, The Seafood Restaurant

PLACES TO EAT | PADSTOW | PL28 8BY

The first restaurant opened by Rick Stein and his wife Jill in 1975, this marks the start of Rick's enterprises in Padstow. The chef now has four restaurants, a bistro, a cafe, a seafood delicatessen, a patisserie shop, a gift shop and a cookery school in town.

This remains the flagship and prides itself on serving fresh quality and locally sourced seafood prepared in front of diners at the seafood bar. The space is large and flooded with light and the restaurant embodies the Stein philosophy of good quality fish cooked simply.

ADDRESS
Riverside
PL28 8BY

PHONE
01841 532700

NEAR HERE
St Petroc's Bistro (p65)
Old Custom House (p49)
Burgers & Fish (p63)

Porthminster Kitchen

PLACES TO EAT | ST. IVES | TR26 1LG

From the team that brought you the Porthminster Beach Café, Porthminster Kitchen in St. Ives continues the theme of celebrating the best of Cornish produce through new and innovative dishes in a modern dining environment. This fresh and popular restaurant is in a prime location on the picturesque St. Ives Harbour.

With a head chef who brings Asian and Mediterranean twists to traditional Cornish seafood, Porthminster Kitchen is something rather special here in St. Ives. The restaurant is a light and airy space that combines rustic wood and modern tiling with more industrial fixtures.

ADDRESS
Wharf Road
TR26 1LG

PHONE
01736 799874

NEAR HERE
Surf Shack Café (p96)
The Balcony Bar (p60)
Mount Zion Coffee (p98)

57 Fore Street

PLACES TO EAT | ST. IVES | TR26 1HE

57 Fore Street is a stylish, warm and welcoming restaurant in St. Ives offering original and irresistible takes on Cornish classics. The good food is complemented by the ornate and playful interior combined with a great location.

Ideal for cream teas, sandwiches and cakes in the daytime, it is just as nice for a special evening meal. Expect curried monkfish tails with cauliflower, vanilla purée or Butternut squash soup with coconut and chilli soup.

ADDRESS

57 Fore Street
TR26 1HE

PHONE

01736 795701

NEAR HERE

The Digey Food Room (p97)

The Allotment Deli (p151)

Olives Cafe (p99)

Cribbs Caribbean Cafe & Bar

PLACES TO EAT | FALMOUTH | TR11 3JE

Cribbs Caribbean Cafe & Bar in Falmouth was founded in 2007 and brings the soul and vibrancy of the Caribbean to this Cornwall fishing port. The delicious and authentic dishes burst with flavour including seafood with a tropical twist, curried jerk chicken and of course ackee and saltfish.

Set up by John Duncan who originates from St Vincent, Cribbs also offers a fine selection of rums, tropical cocktails and even the legendary Jamaican Ting soft drink. The restaurant has a simple Scandinavian design with stylish furniture and decorations in turquoise and orange shades. Transport yourself away to the isles of the Caribbean.

ADDRESS

33 Arwenack Street
TR11 3JE

PHONE

01326 210000

NEAR HERE

Beerwolf Books (p33)

Courtyard Deli & Kitchen (p109)

Espressini Artisan Coffee (p104)

Hub

PLACES TO EAT | ST. IVES | TR26 1LF

Hub is a lively, welcoming and stylish bistro in the heart of town and the go-to place to enjoy cakes and coffee by day and delicious food and cocktails by night. This American-styled bar has a great view of the Wharf and specialises in local rare breed beef burgers, fresh Cornish fish and New York-style free-range pork hot dogs.

Their coffee is fair trade and from sustainable sources and the bar is open until late. The Hub is also behind the pop-up version Hubbox which has opened branches around the south west. Locally baked artisan buns are delivered each morning for their burgers and hot dogs.

ADDRESS

4 Wharf Road
TR26 1LF

PHONE

01736 799099

NEAR HERE

Harbour Fish & Chips (p59)
Surf Shack Café (p96)
The Digey Food Room (p97)

Outlaw's Fish Kitchen

PLACES TO EAT | PORT ISAAC | PL29 3RH

Outlaw's Fish Kitchen serves tapas style plates of local fish and seafood and is the brain child of Michelin-starred chef, Nathan Outlaw. This intimate, bustling little bistro is certainly towards the top of the list of any foodie visiting the area.

This popular bistro takes a modern approach to British cookery with the menu dictated by what the sea and local fisherman produce each day. Sustainability is at the core of what Nathan and his team are doing and they only work with fisherman using low impact fishing methods that preserve our marine environment.

ADDRESS

1 Middle Street
PL29 3RH

PHONE

01208 881183

NEAR HERE

Port Isaac (p22)

The Golden Lion (p41)

Kiln (p134)

Sam's in the City

PLACES TO EAT | TRURO | TR1 2AA

Sam's in the City began 25 years ago and has since opened restaurants in five locations around Cornwall. Now a staple in the South West, the family-run Sam's is known for its good food and support of all things Cornish. This Truro branch is the newest member of the family and is making quite a stir.

Expect fish soup with spiced heritage tomato, pan seared Cornish scallops in garlic butter, noisette and seafood bouillabaisse. The seafoam blue exterior of the restaurant leads to the interior, decked out with music and movie memorabilia including guitars and posters lovingly collected over the years.

ADDRESS

1-2 New Bridge Street
TR1 2AA

PHONE

01872 859819

NEAR HERE

Grounded (p103)

The Old Grammar School (p86)

Truro Cathedral (p169)

Trawlers on the Quay

PLACES TO EAT | **LOOE** | **PL13 1AH**

Known for its salads and its seafood, Trawlers on the Quay in Looe is a comfortable and pleasing spot to sample seafood brought in daily from the fish market just 200m away. With unbridled views over the water, Trawlers is a firm favourite in picturesque Looe, a town with a long history of fishing.

The spacious and airy interior gives a fantastic aspect over the water and if you're lucky you can get a space on a table outside. The menu changes regularly but freshness and originality are always the order of the day. They also provide a chef prepared picnic for guests who plan to cruise the West Looe River.

ADDRESS

The Quay
PL13 1AH

PHONE

01503 269088

NEAR HERE

The Old Sail Loft (p85)

Looe Harbour (p15)

The Blue Peter Inn (p36)

The Watch House

PLACES TO EAT | ST. MAWES | TR2 5DJ

The Watch House in St. Mawes is a contemporary British seafood restaurant with views of the harbour and a menu that strives to provide the best the Cornish coast has to offer. St. Mawes is nestled on the beautiful Roseland Peninsula and is a stunning place for a day trip or overnight stay.

Run by chef Will Gould, The Watch House is dedicated to sustainable seafood supplied by local producers. Expect moules marinière, beetroot cured salmon or a simple crab roll. The Watch House has a comfortable bar with large booths and a light and open dining area upstairs. Takeaway fish and chips are also available.

ADDRESS

1 The Square
TR2 5DJ

PHONE

01326 270038

NEAR HERE

The Golden Lion (p41)

Outlaw's Fish Kitchen (p76)

Kiln (p134)

Port Gaverne Restaurant

PLACES TO EAT | PORT ISAAC | PL29 3SQ

Near to the ancient fishing village of Port Isaac and nestled within a secluded cove lies the award-winning Port Gaverne Hotel. This 17th-century hideaway has a 5 star AA rating and food to match. Awarded the 'top food pub' in Cornwall in 2017, the inn serves "ultra-fresh, coastal, no ego food".

Antique furniture and traditional features create a welcoming atmosphere and an eclectic wine list will keep you well lubricated. Historically, the tiny hamlet of Port Gaverne was a thriving trading port and a flourishing community of boat builders. It now makes a great base from which to explore this beautiful area.

ADDRESS

Port Gaverne
PL29 3SQ

PHONE

01208 880244

NEAR HERE

Outlaw's Fish Kitchen (p76)

The Golden Lion (p41)

Trebarwith Strand (p11)

The Beach at Bude

PLACES TO EAT | BUDE | EX23 8HJ

Head to The Beach overlooking Bude's wonderfully sandy beach for exquisitely presented food in a lively atmosphere. A good place to start is the industrial-style bar with a refreshing cocktail after a long day on the sand, before settling down in the adjacent restaurant for a meal to remember.

Recognised by many as the perfect destination to celebrate a special occasion or treat a loved one, The Beach ticks all the boxes. There are 16 luxurious bedrooms, some of which have balconies overlooking the sea for that idyllic special sunset, service is impeccable and the sea is on your doorstep.

ADDRESS

Summerleaze Crescent
EX23 8HJ

PHONE

01288 389800

NEAR HERE

Summerleaze Beach (p27)

The Castle Bude (p13)

La Bocca Pizza Kitchen (p84)

La Bocca Pizza Kitchen

PLACES TO EAT | BUDE | EX23 8QU

The Neapolitan pizzas from the oven of La Bocca on the Strand in Bude are combined with a modern, industrial interior in this charming little eatery. The team here are passionate about making authentic Italian pizza within their wood fired oven.

A good takeaway pizza is often hard to find when on holiday but you can be be safe in the knowledge that the pizzas from La Bocca are true to their roots. Known for their artisan dough and creative combination of toppings, we recommend the calzone piccante washed down with a cool glass of Peroni.

ADDRESS

24 The Strand

EX23 8QU

PHONE

01288 255855

NEAR HERE

Bleujen Florist (p135)

The Castle Bude (p13)

Summerleaze Beach (p27)

The Old Sail Loft

PLACES TO EAT | LOOE | PL13 1AP

Specialising in steaks and fresh local fish, the Old Sail Loft is one of the oldest buildings in Looe having been built as a quayside warehouse over 450 years ago. A former smuggler's hangout, the Old Sail Loft is today a top restaurant on the quay overlooking the harbour.

This former haunt for smugglers and sea faring men, was once known locally as "The Run" due to its time honoured association with smuggling. Catches are brought in daily to supply their extensive fish menu while the meat and veg are all sourced from local butchers. We recommend sampling a fresh fish finger brioche.

ADDRESS

Quay Street
PL13 1AP

PHONE

01503 262131

NEAR HERE

Trawlers on the Quay (p78)

Looe Harbour (p15)

The Blue Peter Inn (p36)

The Old Grammar School

PLACES TO EAT | TRURO | TR1 2AF

The Old Grammar School is a spacious and quirky restaurant bar that specialises in creative cocktails and tasty tapas in the heart of Truro. A popular spot to unwind with a Mojito and a bowl of Andalou olives, the Old Grammar School is vibrant and fun with a colourful, stripped back aesthetic and friendly staff.

The space is small and intimate which lends to the up beat atmosphere. Portions are generous and prices are fair. Expect crispy squid with sweet chilli & ginger sauce, red thai chicken flatbread and Cornish BBQ pork sliders.

ADDRESS

19 St. Mary's Street
TR1 2AF

PHONE

01872 278559

NEAR HERE

Sam's in the City (p77)

Grounded (p103)

Falmouth Bay Café (p88)

Havener's

PLACES TO EAT | FOWEY | PL23 1AT

Havener's Bar and Grill is located on Fowey's quayside overlooking the calm river Fowey and Polruan. They offer a unique seafood-led menu and are open for breakfast, lunch and dinner. Their menu includes west country mussels, local scallops, gambos and general pub classics.

You can grab a window table or dine outside and watch the ferry and other watercraft bobbing on the water. They sell decent coffee from Brewer and Bean and a selection of St. Austell's award-winning ales. A perfect spot for a sunset tipple and a good night's sleep as rooms are available for those seeking accommodation.

ADDRESS

4 Town Quay
PL23 1AT

PHONE

01726 834591

NEAR HERE

The Old Quay House (p58)

Fowey Harbour (p17)

The Webb Street Co (p138)

Falmouth Bay Seafood Café

PLACES TO EAT | TRURO | TR1 3AF

The award-winning Falmouth Bay Seafood Café is a chic seafood and champagne bar in Truro serving seasonal dishes. Run by Valerie and Vicky, a mother and daughter team, sustainability of the fish they serve is paramount and central to their ethos.

The range of dishes is broad and includes Goan fish curries and squid and chorizo while the the service is attentive and friendly. The vibe is relaxed and there is a south facing garden for dining al fresco. Seek it out, you won't be disappointed.

ADDRESS
53 Castle Street
TR1 3AF

PHONE
01872 278884

NEAR HERE
Hubbox (p61)
Rare Bits (p130)
Truro Cathedral (p169)

The Boathouse

PLACES TO EAT | NEWQUAY | TR7 1HT

With excellent views, this intimate and welcoming quayside eatery in Newquay is a firm favourite with those in the know. The Boathouse has a simple and fresh interior with plenty of outside seating to watch the local fishermen come and go. Pan-seared scallops, roast crab claws in garlic butter and moules mariniere are just a few of the tasty offerings on the menu.

The ethos at this harbour side restaurant is based upon keeping things fresh, simple and local. Tucked beneath the cliffs and right on the beach, the Boathouse is most certainly worth seeking out for a long lunch or a romantic evening meal.

ADDRESS

South Quay Hill
TR7 1HT

PHONE

01637 874062

NEAR HERE

The Harbour Fish & Grill (p70)

Rick Stein, Fistral (p66)

Fistral Beach (p24)

CHAPTER FIVE

CAFÉS &
TEAROOMS

Strong Adolfo's Café

CAFÉS & TEA ROOMS | WADEBRIDGE | PL27 7LR

Strong Adolfos is how a roadside cafe should be. Located on the Atlantic Highway, this Swedish inspired eatery makes an ideal pit stop when touring this beautiful part of Cornwall. This striking building has panoramic glass windows through which you can admire the estuary at Wadebridge.

Inside, the interior is spacious and beautifully decorated with sleek tiling and industrial fittings. This award winning cafe is a hub of creative cookery and the go to venue for a proper cup of coffee. They also specialise in home made cakes, so be sure to sample one while you are there.

ADDRESS

Hawksfield
PL27 7LR

PHONE

01208 816949

NEAR HERE

The Arc Food Store (p141)
Goose Shed (p120)
Circle Gallery (p167)

The Sorting Office

CAFÉS & TEA ROOMS | ST. AGNES | TR5 0ZN

The Sorting Office in St. Agnes is a quirky little coffee shop that has been tastefully refurbished and revamped to provide an essential coffee service to regulars and visitors alike, and few are disappointed. Once the place to post letters, now the place to sup locally roasted beans.

Probably the most eye catching of their wares are their cakes, some impressive rustic creations that taste as good as they look. During the summer months The Sorting Office will sort you out with one of their thirst quenching smoothies and iced lattes.

ADDRESS
Churchtown
TR5 0ZN

PHONE
07807 324088

NEAR HERE
Genki Café (p93)
Q Tearoom (p105)
The Miners Arms (p43)

Genki Café

CAFÉS & TEA ROOMS | ST. AGNES | TR5 0RP

Meaning "health and happiness" in Japanese, Genki's atmosphere, ambience and setting certainly help to nurture those benefits. This little shack close to the beach in St. Agnes provides nourishment throughout the day and you can enjoy a moment's peace and good eats in their tiered Zen garden.

Breakfast ranges from Sunday bacon baps to slightly more healthy acai bowls and smoothies, lunch is a myriad of salads and sandwiches and themed summer evenings include tapas, sushi and fine cocktails. A chilled out beachside mini gem, Genki is a welcome stopping point on the way to the sea and a destination in its own right.

ADDRESS

Quay Road
TR5 0RP

PHONE

01872 555858

NEAR HERE

Q Tearoom (p105)

The Sorting Office (p92)

The Miners Arms (p43)

Surf Shack Café

CAFÉS & TEA ROOMS | ST. IVES | TR26 1LG

The elevated Surf Shack Café boasts one of the best views of the stunning St. Ives Harbour. On the menu is a varied selection of German treats such as Kasekrainer and Tiroler Strudel, filled French crepes and more commonly found panini's and cream teas. This is a swell café to chill out in as the friendly staff are very welcoming and laid back.

The Surf Shack Café's distressed crate panelling, eclectic plants and flowers, colourful artwork and mismatched furniture provide a cosy atmosphere. Grab a slice of cake and cup of coffee and watch the boats go by.

ADDRESS

Wharf Road
TR26 1LG

PHONE

07905 998808

NEAR HERE

57 Fore Street (p73)

Hub (p75)

Harbour Fish & Chips (p59)

The Digey Food Room

CAFÉS & TEA ROOMS | ST. IVES | TR26 1HR

A welcome stop after exploring the beautiful St. Ives is the Digey, aptly named after the quiet cobbled street it sits on. Both a café and luxury food emporium known for its (nearly) all day Cornish breakfasts, healthy lunch options, cakes and quiches as well as excellent coffee.

Their food shop is the go-to place for high quality preserves, sauces, biscuits and chutneys for both locals and visitors alike. They even provide "Digey beach picnic boxes"- an excellent idea that means you can just rock up, grab your hamper and hit the sand.

ADDRESS

6 The Digey
TR26 1HR

PHONE

01736 799600

NEAR HERE

Ferrell S H & Son (p130)

Mount Zion Coffee (p98)

Fish Pye Pottery (p128)

Mount Zion Coffee

CAFÉS & TEA ROOMS | ST. IVES | TR26 1PZ

Forget snazzy cakes and eating etiquette, Mount Zion is all about coffee. Set just off the harbour of St. Ives, this old woodsman's workshop has been transformed into a top class coffee shop.

Their slogan states your drink isn't rushed, which is totally plausible when you see how much effort goes into each coffee. Sit with one of Tunnocks famous teacakes or a caramel wafer bar and watch the harbour in all its splendour with a perfect brew.

ADDRESS
Wharf Road
TR26 1PZ

PHONE
01736 888419

NEAR HERE
Penwith Gallery (p162)
Fish Pye Pottery (p128)
Olives Cafe (p99)

Olives Cafe

CAFÉS & TEA ROOMS | ST. IVES | TR26 1NX

Olives café is the ideal hang-out for any cream tea and cake lover and the small elevated room inside and a scattering of tables out front are generally filled by those with a sweet tooth. The counter as you enter displays mouth watering delicacies and the vibrant eye-catching exterior lures you in.

This area of St. Ives is a touch quieter than the rest and has plenty of galleries and studios to explore. Olives Café is well suited to get the energy levels back up before heading over towards The Island and the sandy Porthgwidden Beach.

ADDRESS

Island Square
TR26 1NX

PHONE

07875 585759

NEAR HERE

Fish Pye Pottery (p128)

Mount Zion Coffee (p98)

Penwith Gallery (p162)

The Honey Pot

CAFÉS & TEA ROOMS | PENZANCE | TR18 4BU

The Honey Pot has been serving customers on and off for more than 100 years and remains a popular place to stop for a cup of tea while exploring Penzance. This old teashop has been lovingly restored and now serves comfort food with a smile.

Located in the historic part of town, its windows on two sides provide a great viewpoint for life going by. The Honey Pot's history and longevity in the town create a sense of connection with days gone by and you can expect a warm welcome and hearty, homely dishes. This is the perfect place to warm up after a dip in the Jubilee Pool or the sea.

ADDRESS

5 Parade Street
TR18 4BU

PHONE

01736 368686

NEAR HERE

No.56 (p73)

The Cornish Barn (p64)

The Granary (p152)

Jam

CAFÉS & TEA ROOMS | FALMOUTH | TR11 2AD

Is it a café or is it a record shop? Well it's a bit of both and more. Jam is an eclectic mix of vinyl, coffee art, books and muffins in a shop that could be the definition of "shabby chic". Nestled in Falmouth Old Town, Jam is not like a music store you'd find in the city but the retro shambolic atmosphere is all part of its charm.

Music and good coffee pair up like the seaside and ice-cream. Jam serve them up in style with the latest and greatest vinyl backing soundtrack. A cool place to hang out and spend a few bob on keeping vinyl alive.

ADDRESS

32 High Street
TR11 2AD

PHONE

01326 211722

NEAR HERE

Stones Bakery (p157)
The Chintz Symposium (p37)
The Falmouth Pottery (p123)

Rock Pool Café

CAFÉS & TEA ROOMS | MOUSEHOLE | TR19 6PT

The Rock Pool Café looks out over the intoxicating ocean and is the perfect spot to enjoy moreish cakes and light lunches. On a fine day we recommend you grab a bench outside and enjoy the heat of the sun and comforting sea breeze while satisfying your tastebuds.

Inside, you can browse through a selection of locally made ceramic goods from Welbeck Tiles. Combine your refreshments with a stroll down to the Rock Pool beneath the café and hunt for crustaceans and sea treasures and dip your feet into the cool waters.

ADDRESS
The Parade
TR19 6PT

PHONE
01736 732645

NEAR HERE
Sandpiper Gallery (p171)
2 Fore Street Restaurant (p51)
Ship Inn (p44)

Grounded

CAFÉS & TEA ROOMS | TRURO | TR1 2AA

Small but well proportioned, Grounded serves up tasty treats such as falafels, fresh sandwiches, pastries and quiches to brighten up your lunchtime. On the grind is local Olfactory Coffee which hits the senses as soon as you walk through the door.

Get your hot brew fix and get friendly with the locals on one of the small tables. You can also take away a bag of roasted goodness and enjoy the beans at home. This is a welcoming and cosy café, with lots to offer, a very good choice for pause when exploring the lovely city of Truro.

ADDRESS

5 New Bridge Street
TR1 2AA

PHONE

01872 272277

NEAR HERE

Sam's in the City (p77)

The Old Grammar School (p86)

Truro Arts Company (p132)

Espressini Artisan Coffee

CAFÉS & TEA ROOMS | FALMOUTH | TR11 3PW

Espressini is a speciality coffee shop and kitchen, based in Falmouth. This is the birthplace of the Espressini brand which has been creating quality coffee since 2011. One of three Espressini, Falmouth is their flagship store and has been listed in The Independent's Top 50 speciality coffee shops.

Owner Rupert Ellis and his team are passionate about the provenance of the beans they serve and make an effort to build relationships with growers and farmers around the world. The coffee shop decor is eclectic vintage with floral wallpaper and unique wrought iron tables.

ADDRESS

39 Killigrew Street
TR11 3PW

PHONE

01326 236582

NEAR HERE

Cribbs Caribbean Cafe & Bar (p74)

Beerwolf Books (p33)

Falmouth Art Gallery (p166)

Q Tearoom, Studio & Gallery

CAFÉS & TEA ROOMS | ST. AGNES | TR5 0RS

Tucked into a quiet corner of St. Agnes, Q Tea Room & Gallery is a cheerful and welcoming café with walls adorned with the work of local artists. Formerly the site of the village petrol station, the location is now home to more glitter and baubles than oil and windscreen wipers.

Near to Trevaunance Cove, this quirky tea room serves Cornish grown tea and high teas alongside traditional cream teas. Savoury dishes include spicy parsnip soup, sausage buns & bacon baps. This cafe makes a great little getaway from the summer crowds.

ADDRESS

Quay Road
TR5 0RS

PHONE

01872 857045

NEAR HERE

The Sorting Office (p92)

Genki Café (p93)

The Miners Arms (p43)

Scoff Troff Cafe

CAFÉS & TEA ROOMS | ST. IVES | TR26 1RZ

Easily found by the bright orange pig on the shop front, Scoff Troff in the St. Ives marketplace is a vibrant cafe serving delicious breakfasts, lunches and sharing platters. The produce is all locally sourced, the bread is baked at a bakery around the corner each morning.

Born out of a love of food and travel, Scoff Troff brings the vibrancy of global street food and exotic dishes to St. Ives. Food is hearty, prices reasonable and portions generous. We recommend the hot chocolate with marshmallows and a scone with cream and jam for an indulgent afternoon. Dogs are welcome.

ADDRESS

Market Place
TR26 1RZ

PHONE

01736 797341

NEAR HERE

Alba Restaurant (p62)
The Allotment Deli (p151)
Porthminster Gallery (p163)

Courtyard Deli & Kitchen

CAFÉS & TEA ROOMS | FALMOUTH | TR11 3AZ

Courtyard Deli in Falmouth sell a fine array of delectable dishes from its cosy upstairs café where worldly flavours can be sampled in a friendly and bright setting. The downstairs deli offers a diverse selection of produce from different countries and cultures, both to have in and take away.

Muffins, scones and cakes are baked on the premises, and there are all your regular deli items such as cheeses and chutneys to accompany them. The deli produce covers a wide range of meats and salads, and pre-packed ingredients from around the globe, each carefully sourced for quality and originality.

ADDRESS

2 Bells Court
TR11 3AZ

PHONE

01326 727007

NEAR HERE

Beerwolf Books (p33)

Baker Tom's (p118)

Cribbs Caribbean Cafe (p74)

The Front Room

CAFÉS & TEA ROOMS | PENZANCE | TR18 2LG

Bathed in natural light, the Front Room in Penzance is an airy and fresh eatery that serves a toothsome mix of traditional and hip dishes and drinks. The memorable breakfast ranges from acai bowls to doughnuts and the classic full English. They also offer excellent veggie alternatives, making it a regular morning stop-off for all.

The Front Room is shabby chic in style, complete with comfy mismatching chairs, wood flooring, sanded white walls and decorative additions. On a summer's day, grab a luxury milkshake and slurp through the straw to rediscover your inner child

ADDRESS

83 Market Jew Street
TR18 2LG

PHONE

01736 448681

NEAR HERE

The Granary (p152)

The Honey Pot (p100)

No.56 (p73)

Blue Tomato

CAFÉS & TEA ROOMS | ROCK | PL27 6LD

You can find Blue Tomato in Rock, a beautiful beachside town a short ferry trip from Padstow. First impressions are a café with great views and then as the food starts coming out of the kitchen smelling divine you realise you're in for a treat.

The team at Blue Tomato are passionate about ensuring the customer feels welcome and the service is second to none. The interior window wall opens up to unrivalled views over the turquoise waters of the River Camel to Padstow beyond. Here you can expect to find many of your favourite dishes cooked to perfection.

Duchy of Cornwall Nursery

CAFÉS & TEA ROOMS | LOSTWITHIEL | PL22 0HW

The Duchy of Cornwall Plant Nursery in Lostwithiel is a high-quality plant emporium with an award-winning café and homeware shop. Sporting wonderful views across the Fowey valley to Restormel Castle, the Duchy Plant Nursery sells top shrubs and blooms and the café serves food from 9am until 4.30pm daily.

Settle down in the café or terrace and browse the daily papers or gardening books with a decent sandwich, homemade bread or a proper Cornish cream tea. The calm and comfortable interior complement the experience and the warm welcome from the staff is the icing on the cake.

ADDRESS

Cott Road
PL22 0HW

PHONE

01208 872668

NEAR HERE

Black Dog Antiques (p131)

Bellamama Deli (p142)

Eden Project (p12)

Town & Country Kitchen

CAFÉS & TEA ROOMS | ST. COLUMB | TR9 6AJ

The Town & Country Kitchen Café is a chilled and recently renovated, independent coffee shop and café in the uniquely named village of St Columb Major.

This cosy and quirky cafe feels like a home from home with a myriad of rooms and wiggly staircases to navigate. Breakfasts are hearty and everything is home made. The Town and Country Kitchen has created quite a buzz in the town so it can get busy. Worth seeking out this new addition to the Cornwall culinary scene.

ADDRESS
61 Fore Street
TR9 6AJ

PHONE
01637 889995

NEAR HERE
Jamie Oliver's Fifteen (p53)
Catch Seafood, Bar & Grill (p67)
The Harbour Fish & Grill (p70)

Tatams

CAFÉS & TEA ROOMS | PORTSCATHO | TR2 5HQ

Basically located in the sea, Tatams in Portscatho is the number-one spot for a shot of finest Olfactory coffee with unblemished views of gorgeous coastline. Perhaps not the most luxurious of places to sit on a rainy day as there is no indoor seating, but pure gold when the suns out.

Why not walk a few miles along Cornwall's dramatic coastal path and then pause here for a cheese and ham filled croissant, breakfast pasty, flapjack or custard tart. Skim a few stones in the sea then hunt for sea creatures amidst the rocks.

ADDRESS
The Slip-Way
TR2 5HQ

PHONE
01872 581894

NEAR HERE
The Harbour Gallery (p170)
Portscatho (p16)
The Watch House (p79)

Yummy Scrummy Bakery

CAFÉS & TEA ROOMS | PAR | PL24 2AQ

Yummy Scrummy Bakery is a cosy little cafe located within the village and fishing port of Par which has a direct mainline railway station to Paddington. The bakery is family run by folk who are passionate about good quality food.

A selection of artisan breads are baked daily without additives, improve or stabilisers and their cakes are homemade with organic flour. If you are local and love your bread, they even run an artisan loyalty bread club. Seek it out and treat yourself to one of their handmade Cornish chocolates.

ADDRESS
23 Eastcliffe Road
PL24 2AQ

PHONE
01726 813565

NEAR HERE
Eden Project (p12)
Readymoney Cove (p14)
Fowey Harbour (p17)

Baker Tom's

CAFÉS & TEA ROOMS | FALMOUTH | TR11 3DR

Set up by Tom Hazzeldine at the age of 29, Baker Tom's in Falmouth is one of four outlets of this award-winning chain of Cornish bakeries. Tom's focuses on fresh, specialty breads, pastries and cakes using traditional baking methods and only the best organic ingredients.

Not only a bakery for artisan sourdough loaves and wholemeal cobs you can also enjoy pancakes, pizza and pastries in their Falmouth café. We suggest trying the parmesan and red onion loaf or one of their croissants made with 100% Cornish butter. Any left over produce from each day goes to the homeless.

ADDRESS

10C Church Street
TR11 3DR

PHONE

01326 318221

NEAR HERE

Beerwolf Books (p33)

Courtyard Deli & Kitchen (p109)

National Maritime Museum (p161)

CHAPTER SIX

SHOPPING

Goose Shed

SHOPPING | WADEBRIDGE | PL27 7LR

Situated near Hawksfield on the North Coast of Cornwall, the Goose Shed is a discerning hipster's delight specialising in original vintage interior designs and reclaimed decorative pieces. The store has an ever-changing, eclectic collection of items chosen for their soul and style.

Goose Shed is creatively directed by Jean-Paul Kuhnzack-Richards who has over 25 years of experience in architectural and interiors furniture and arts. If it is raining and you are stuck for inspiration, head here to pick up some original interior items for your home and then have lunch at Strong Adolfos next door.

ADDRESS

Hawkshead

PL27 7LR

PHONE

01208 813863

NEAR HERE

Strong Adolfos Cafe (p91)

The Arc Food Store (p141)

Circle Contemporary Gallery (p167)

Notes

Tried our app?

bestofengland.com/app

Toro Studio

SHOPPING | FALMOUTH | TR11 2BY

Toro in Falmouth is dedicated to exploring the healing properties and values of plants and the proprietor is open to sharing interesting advice on growing and caring for botanicals in your own home. For sale are an excellent array of exceptional plants and botanical equipment and wares.

Toro also hold regular workshops for all levels and botanical interests, including terrarium building and botanical drawing. Their knowledge and experience can provide essential insights into house plants and other exotics. Set in the quirky Old Brewery Yard, Toro is an original and attractive concept.

ADDRESS

Old Brewery Yard
TR11 2BY

PHONE

07528 562737

NEAR HERE

The Chintz Symposium (p37)

Stones Bakery (p157)

Jam (p101)

The Falmouth Pottery

SHOPPING | FALMOUTH | TR11 3AU

Falmouth Pottery is home to the renowned artist Michel Francois and his kilned creations. His working studio displays a fine selection of his pottery, all of which is for sale and includes elegant and classic thrown pots, vases and cups and some fine porcelain pieces.

Michel Francois' work is functional and practical, yet captures the beauty of simple lines and colour. Michel uses feldspar, Cornish stone, marble, and wood from local trees, such as chestnut, ash, and beech to enhance and experiment with. Tableware designed by Michel can also been found at the Eden Project.

ADDRESS

12 Webber Street
TR11 3AU

PHONE

01326 211663

NEAR HERE

Falmouth Art Gallery (p166)

Jam (p101)

Courtyard Deli & Kitchen (p109)

Johns Wine & Spirits Specialists

SHOPPING | ST. IVES | TR26 1HW

In the family since 1894, Johns Wine & Spirits has transformed from a grocers to one of Cornwall's most extensive stockists of wine, spirits and craft beers. Their range covers local gin suppliers to rare and exquisite imports from all over the globe

The discerning selection of Johns Wine and Spirits results in only the finest and most interesting liquor being available in the store, ideally placed in central downtown St. Ives. However, you can now order any of their stock via their extensive new website shop.

ADDRESS

75 Fore Street
TR26 1HW

PHONE

01736 795797

NEAR HERE

Ferrell S H & Son (p130)

The Digey Food Room (p97)

Porthminster Kitchen (p72)

No. 56

SHOPPING | PENZANCE | TR18 4AW

Entering No.56 you are immediately welcomed by clean walls and well displayed crafts, homewares and gifts. Everything seems to have been allocated its own space in this minimalistic shop where you can easily browse for something tasteful, for a present or to decorate your own home.

Seeking out innovative and original designers, the owner (curator) Carole Elsworth has a keen eye for aesthetics and a love of simplicity and attention to detail. The product lines often change, but you'll be sure to find fine objects in wood, linen, clay and natural weave whenever you're lucky enough to visit.

ADDRESS

14 Chapel Street
TR18 4AW

PHONE

01736 366293

NEAR HERE

The Honey Pot (p100)

The Cornish Barn (p64)

Ian Lentern Butchers (p147)

Fish Pye Pottery

SHOPPING | ST. IVES | TR26 1NL

Fish Pye Pottery is an eclectic and welcoming pottery studio and shop that is located in the renowned seaside town of St. Ives. Inside Fish Pye Pottery, you will be greeted with shelves stacked with colourful, handcrafted works that are both interesting and practical.

Laura will often be sitting behind the wheel, sculpting her latest creation. Most of the artwork and pots use bold natural colours and would make an excellent gift or souvenir from this arty town. Many of the local businesses use the pottery in their eateries and shops as it's both striking and original.

ADDRESS

47 Back Road East
TR26 1NL

PHONE

01736 793863

NEAR HERE

Penwith Gallery (p162)

Olives Cafe (p99)

Mount Zion Coffee (p98)

The Mousehole

SHOPPING | MOUSEHOLE | TR19 6PL

The Mousehole is a charming gift shop nestled in one of Cornwall's most picturesque harbours and within a charming waterfront cottage. From the outside, you would think that there isn't much to be seen inside but the gallery space is deceptively large.

Inside, you will find the colourful kitchenware and crockery, landscape paintings by local artists and all kinds of trinkets and presents to take home. This fishing village is a magnet for art lovers and the Mousehole is a firm favourite among those who visit this dramatic region of the Cornish coastline.

ADDRESS

Quay Street
TR19 6PL

PHONE

01736 731893

NEAR HERE

The Rock Pool Cafe (102)

Sandpiper Gallery (p171)

2 Fore Street Restaurant (p51)

Rare Bits

SHOPPING | TRURO | TR1 2AZ

Rare Bits is a retro inspired homeware and lifestyle shop located in the restored Grade II listed Peoples Palace. This lively business is bursting with personality and an excellent collection of upcycled items from the 1920s through to the 1970s including old rocking horses, school desks, guitars to all sorts of bric a brac. This eclectic store makes for a unique and enjoyable shopping experience.

The building itself is fascinating, with its cob and exposed beams it is full of character. If you are looking for a spot of colour to brighten up your home then be sure to head here.

ADDRESS
Peoples Palace
TR1 2AZ

PHONE
01872 858021

NEAR HERE
Royal Cornwall Museum (p168)
Truro Arts Company (p132)
Hubbox (p61)

Black Dog Antiques & Interiors

SHOPPING | LOSTWITHIEL | PL22 0BS

Black Dog Antiques resides in the Duchy Palace, one of Lostwithiel's oldest buildings, and combines traditional country furniture with eclectic and interesting antique pieces from the 17th to the 20th centuries. Not just the standard stuffy and dusty antiques shop, the Black Dog strives to be different, from the décor to the quirky collection.

Lostwithiel is known as the "antiques capital of Cornwall" and to stand out from the crowd the owners decided to brand their shop as something a bit different, and chose to name it after their (sadly passed away) loyal shop companion, Dusty, the black dog.

ADDRESS

Quay Street
PL22 0BS

PHONE

01208 872909

NEAR HERE

Bellamama Deli (p142)

Duchy of Cornwall (p112)

Eden Project (p12)

Truro Arts Company

SHOPPING | TRURO | TR1 2SJ

One of the largest arts and crafts suppliers in the South West, the Truro Arts Company is not just an art store but also an exhibition space and a café, for coffee and cake stops. Truro Arts Company has been in business for over 25 years and has built a loyal following. The exhibition space hosts a rolling programme of work from popular and upcoming local artists.

They also run a series of creative workshops for children to let their imaginations run riot and life drawing classes for adults to escape. Truro Arts Company is truly the arts hub of Cornwall. If you are planning on doing any painting while in Cornwall then this is the destination for you.

ADDRESS

26 River Street
TR1 2SJ

PHONE

01872 240567

NEAR HERE

Royal Cornwall Museum (p168)

Falmouth Bay Cafe (p88)

Hubbox (p61)

Armstrong & Wing

SHOPPING | ST. IVES | TR26 1AH

Armstrong & Wing is a tiny interior and antique shop in St. Ives selling hand-painted wooden furniture, tableware and artwork for the home. Bursting with colour and creativity, Armstrong & Wing is one of St. Ives many creative small businesses.

All the wooden creations are hand painted and crafted in their home in the hills just outside St.Ives. Inside the shop you'll find an ever-changing collection of crafts in an array of colours, along with art by Janine Wing and other gifts and accessories such as bunting, coasters and placemats.

ADDRESS

10 St. Andrew's Street
TR26 1AH

PHONE

01736 797985

NEAR HERE

Porthminster Gallery (p163)
Scoff Troff Cafe (p108)
Alba Restaurant (p62)

Kiln

SHOPPING | PORT ISAAC | PL29 3RH

Kiln is a family run shop in pretty Port Isaac selling painted bone china and textiles of Sue Pullin. Sue has been designing and painting for over 25 years, and the shop gets its name from her kilns in the studio out back. Kiln also stocks various Scandinavian homeware, as well as unique gifts sourced from all over Cornwall.

The white bone china is all made in England and comes from potteries in Stoke on Trent with their designs being inked by hand on site, before firing (out the back). If you are looking for a souvenir that is a bit different then be sure to stop by.

ADDRESS
No 3 Middle Street
PL29 3RH

PHONE
01208 880578

NEAR HERE
Port Isaac (p22)

Outlaw's Fish Kitchen (p76)

The Golden Lion (p41)

Bleujen Florist

SHOPPING | BUDE | EX23 8JL

First set up in 2008, Bleujen in Bude is an award-winning florist offering innovative flower designs. Erica Tippet, Bleujen's florist owner, has a passion for flower creations and the results are apparent in the five awards won at the RHS Chelsea Flower show over the years.

Bleujen is Cornish for flower and the shop is modern, contemporary and bright. Bleujen is now a firm fixture in the Bude community and fits right into this arty hamlet beside a picturesque canal.

ADDRESS
7 Belle Vue
EX23 8JL

PHONE
01288 354606

NEAR HERE
La Bocca Pizza Kitchen (p84)
The Castle Bude (p13)
Summerleaze Beach (p27)

The Webb Street Company

SHOPPING | FOWEY | PL23 1AP

The Webb Street Company is a craft and gift shop with a focus on products that are simply but beautifully designed. The shop stocks artwork, jewellery and tableware that has been sourced carefully to fit in with their ethos, with Cornwall and with the influence of the sea.

Founded in 2013, the Webb Street Company was created out of a love for well-designed everyday objects that stand the test of time. Classic enamel tableware, creative and original embroidery, and quirky handmade dolls make unique souvenirs to take home from your Cornish adventure.

ADDRESS
2 Webb Street
PL23 1AP

PHONE
01726 833838

NEAR HERE
Havener's (p87)
Quay Bakery (p156)
Fowey Harbour (p17)

CHAPTER SEVEN

FOOD
SHOPS

Ferrell S H & Son

FOOD SHOPS | ST. IVES | TR26 1HW

Ferrell & Son has been serving fresh baked Cornish treats to St. Ives residents and visitors for four generations and the traditional bakery produces fresh breads, brownies, pasties and cakes daily. In 2017 they won the coveted "Ultimate Pasty Maker" award, coinciding with the World Pasty Championships at the Eden Project.

Good old fashioned friendly service is the order of the day and, as a result, locals proudly claim the baker is the best in St. Ives. If you only try one pasty in Cornwall, then make it a genuine one from Ferrells.

ADDRESS
64 Fore Street
TR26 1HW

PHONE
01736 797703

NEAR HERE
Johns Wine Specialist (p124)
The Digey Food Room (p97)
Porthminster Kitchen (p72)

The Arc Speciality Food Store

FOOD SHOPS | WADEBRIDGE | PL27 7LR

The Arc Speciality Food Store is a new and exciting edition to the collective shopping gallery of Hawksfield in Wadebridge. Among the other innovative businesses on site, The Arc sources independent food products from all around the world, including gluten and dairy free.

The name Arc refers to the countries along the Atlantic coast that need some economic support, fitting given the location of this shop on the Atlantic Highway. The shop's stock, as you might imagine, is an eclectic range of local and international products, with pickles, preserves, tins, jars and packets of rarities.

ADDRESS
Atlantic Highway
PL27 7LR

PHONE
01208 816634

NEAR HERE
Circle Gallery (p167)
Strong Adolfos Cafe (p91)
Goose Shed (p120)

Bellamama Deli

FOOD SHOPS | LOSTWITHIEL | PL22 0BL

This modest-sized Deli in Lostwithiel stocks a good selection of foods both local and from further afield. Their Origin coffee is roasted locally and they stock artisan cheese produced on the North Cornish coast. You can also find a fine selection of locally cured ham along with good quality Italian and other continental charcuterie meats.

A great choice of sourdough loaves and other breads are imported daily from the Quay bakery in nearby Fowey. Bellamama also transforms itself from a deli food outlet into a pizzeria on a Friday night, so you can dine out as well as grab your lunch munch.

ADDRESS

24 Fore Street
PL22 0BL

PHONE

01208 872524

NEAR HERE

Black Dog Antiques (p131)

Duchy of Cornwall (p112)

Yummy Scrummy Bakery (p115)

Stevenson Newlyn

FOOD SHOPS | NEWLYN | TR18 5HB

Stevenson Newlyn is an impressive fishmongers that catches, lands and sells the finest fresh fish from Newlyn harbour in the far southwest of Cornwall. With over 100 years experience they are certainly in the know and have Britain's largest privately owned fleet of boats bringing in the daily goods.

Their successful wholesale fish business is complemented by the Stevenson Newlyn store, where the friendly team will provide advice and info on the daily haul. They also operate a first class delivery system if you are unable to get to the store in person.

ADDRESS

Harbour Offices
TR18 5HB

PHONE

01736 362982

NEAR HERE

Trelawney Fish & Deli (p155)

Mackerel Sky Seafood Bar (p57)

The Rock Pool Cafe (102)

Buttermilk

FOOD SHOPS | PADSTOW | PL28 8AW

Stepping into Buttermilk you'll be greeting by the sweet scent of the craft confectioners hard at work. Traditional methods of using mighty copper pans over open flames are still in place and have been since Buttermilk began 50 years ago. They now create over 70 delicious flavours to tantalise your tastebuds.

Inside the Padstow shop, the selection includes smooth fudge, crumbly fudge, brittle, honeycomb and much more. Delighting customers since 1964, Buttermilk has gone from strength to strength with strong branding, great ingredients and the best fudge in town.

ADDRESS

1 Chapel Court
PL28 8AW

PHONE

01841 532542

NEAR HERE

The Seafood Restaurant (p71)

St Petroc's Bistro (p65)

Old Custom House (p49)

Cornish Mill and Bakehouse

FOOD SHOPS | NEWQUAY | TR8 5EQ

The Cornish Mill and Bakehouse is a family farming enterprise that grows and mills its own flour, ready for baking. It first began as a side-product to subsidise the farm and has expanded due to demand and enjoyment. They now run a homely converted milking parlour as a bakery in Saint Newlyn, not too far from Newquay.

In the Bakehouse they sell all of their goods including pasties and pies, bread and buns, cakes and slices as well as serving hot drinks and light lunch bites. You can also buy preserves, veg and a few cheeses. The Bakehouse runs partly as a cafe so you can have the pleasure of eating in.

ADDRESS

Holywell Road
TR8 5EQ

PHONE

01637 830958

NEAR HERE

Fistral Beach (p24)

The Boathouse (p89)

Rick Stein, Fistral (p66)

Healey's Cornish Cyder Farm

FOOD SHOPS | TRURO | TR4 9LW

With the focus on apples and fine flavours, Healey's newly refurbished Cornish Cyder Farm makes for a memorable day out for all the family. Tours run throughout the day allowing visitors to see the cider making process and take a tractor ride around the 100 acres of farm land and 20 acres of mature orchards.

Children can pet the farm animals while Mum and Dad enjoy their free cider samples as well as Cornwall's first Apple Brandy for over 300 years. Traditional Cornish cream tea is also served at the Mowhay restaurant.

ADDRESS

Penhallow
TR4 9LW

PHONE

01872 573356

NEAR HERE

The Miners Arms (p43)
The Sorting Office (p92)
Genki Café (p93)

Ian Lentern Butchers

FOOD SHOPS | PENZANCE | TR18 4AJ

With over four generations of experience in the trade, Ian Lentern Butchers is a family run business that supplies much of Penzance with high quality, locally sourced meat. This spacious and modern butchers offers an extensive selection of fresh local meats and poultry.

Harking back to the days when a local butchers was the first stop for all your meat needs, the traditional and friendly approach of the butcher's staff bring years of experience to your purchasing, and the deli area also provides a fine selection of cooked products such as pasties, pies and scotch eggs.

ADDRESS

1 Chapel Street
TR18 4AJ

PHONE

01736 363061

NEAR HERE

The Honey Pot (p100)

No.56 (p73)

The Cornish Barn (p64)

Lobbs Farm Shop

FOOD SHOPS | ST. EWE | PL26 6EN

Lobbs Farm Shop at Heligan is a Cornish business retailing the best food from the countryside. The three farming brothers, Terry, Ian and Richard Lobb each own a farm, which supplies beef, lamb and fresh vegetables direct to the Farm Shop. The beef and lamb are born and raised on the farm where the animals graze traditional pastures and meadows.

Passionate about selling the best of Cornish Produce, Lobbs aims to produce and sell quality food with a known provenance and is an excellent place to buy the best local meat in the area. Cheeses, pies, preserves along with fruit and vegetables are also available.

ADDRESS
Heligan
PL26 6EN

PHONE
01726 844411

NEAR HERE
Lost Gardens of Heligan (p26)

Mevagissey (p30)

The Sharksfin (p46)

The Allotment Deli

FOOD SHOPS | ST. IVES | TR26 1HE

An innovative concept nestled in the midst of St. Ives, The Allotment Deli offers very local produce from farms, bakeries, cheesemakers and of course allotments in the area. The veg, fruit, meat, cheese and bread are all fresh and they'll even deliver to your door for free once a week (if you live relatively locally).

The deli also stocks a host of homemade pies, pasties, salads, cakes and other treats, perfect for a walk along the coast path to Zennor or a sandy beach picnic. This is truly local food, sourced from honest locals, serving decent fruit and veg back to the locals and the occasional visitor.

ADDRESS

30a Fore Street
TR26 1HE

PHONE

01736 794578

NEAR HERE

The Balcony Bar (p60)

57 Fore Street (p73)

Porthminster Kitchen (p72)

The Granary

FOOD SHOPS | PENZANCE | TR18 2SN

The Granary is a vibrant and abundant vegetarian food emporium, and the ideal place in Penzance to stock up on fruits, veggies, bread and much more. They stock a wide range of vegetarian, vegan and gluten-free whole-food dishes, which are complemented by healthy takeaway salads from the deli counter.

The bright turquoise exterior and colourful display of fresh fruits and vegetables outside lure you into the well-stocked shop. The Granary was first established in 1976 and has over the years honed its range to sell nutritionally first-rate foods.

ADDRESS

15D Causewayhead
TR18 2SN

PHONE

01736 361869

NEAR HERE

The Front Room (p110)

The Honey Pot (p100)

No.56 (p73)

Boscastle Farm Shop

FOOD SHOPS | BOSCASTLE | PL35 0HH

Boscastle Farm Shop sits literally on the Cornish coastal path and looks out over an epic seascape and farmland where their pedigree cattle can often be seen grazing. Their deli and shop sells the best cuts of home reared award-winning beef, lamb and pork as well as flavoursome quiches, pies and cakes.

Everything is reasonably priced and you can sample the same deli produce transformed into all-day breakfasts and homely lunches in their bright cafe. Catch a breath of fresh air and dine outside with the views, followed by a stroll to the cliff edge where you can often spot seals and peregrine falcons.

ADDRESS
Hillsborough Farm
PL35 0HH

PHONE
01840 250827

NEAR HERE
Boscastle (p10)
Museum of Witchcraft and Magic (p160)
The Mill House Inn (p48)

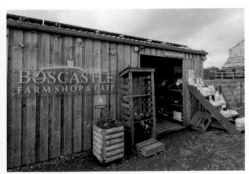

BEST OF ENGLAND
INSPIRING DISCOVERY

About Best of England
Honest Recommendations & Hidden Gems

What is Best of England?

Best of England is a curated collection of travel recommendations. Each one is researched and has been visited and photographed by a member of the Best of England team.

Authenticity & integrity

None of the businesses in this travel guide have paid to be included and we visit every business that we recommend. This guide is based on our own experiences and opinions. We think honesty is a really important part of what we are trying to achieve.

Local knowledge is key

We believe there is nothing better than local knowledge. That's why we speak to the people that live there to find out where to go.

Quality is everything

Quality is behind everything we do and we will never compromise on the recommendations we make. We worry about the details from the thickness of the paper to the size of each font we use and we hope that this effort is reflected in the quality of our products.

Great content comes first

We use our photography to tell a story for each of the businesses we recommend. We want to bring each one to life and inspire our readers to visit themselves.

Tell us what you think

We are always on the look out for ways to improve. Feedback is really important to us in order to make the best product possible. If you have any suggestions or feedback then please let us know via email to **info@bestofengland.com**

Trelawney Fish & Deli

FOOD SHOPS | NEWLYN | TR18 5HW

Trelawney Fish & Deli was established in 1982 and is a family owned fishmonger and delicatessen in Newlyn. They have a wealth of experience and a well-earned reputation for the freshest fish in the area. The fine array of fresh catches all have a story to tell and the staff at Trelawney are happy to elaborate.

The delicatessen also offers a selection of drinks and preserves alongside fish, and they also mail goods throughout Europe. The landed fish are rushed to the packaging area, where they are packed and dispatched in chilled, insulated boxes.

ADDRESS

78 Strand
TR18 5HW

PHONE

01736 332043

NEAR HERE

Stevenson Newlyn (p143)

Mackerel Sky Seafood Bar (p57)

Jubilee Pool (p25)

Quay Bakery

FOOD SHOPS | FOWEY | PL23 1AH

The smell of artisan cakes, breads and other bakes sweeten Fowey's air like a dawn chorus each morning. Savouries, iced buns and other floury treats adorn the shop front and the Quay Bakery both sticks to its staples and offers new creations regularly.

The bakery has been a huge success and word has spread through Fowey about its mission to provide the people with the real fresh baked bread they desire. In 2015 the bakery relocated to Fore Street, from where they plan to bake for Fowey and its many visitors for years to come.

ADDRESS

37 Fore Street
PL23 1AH

PHONE

01726 833263

NEAR HERE

Fowey Harbour (p17)

The Webb Street Company (p138)

Havener's (p87)

Stones Bakery

FOOD SHOPS | FALMOUTH | TR11 2AD

Stones Bakery on the old High Street in Falmouth is one of those places you talk to others about. The extensive range of affordable homemade cakes, pastries, freshly baked bread, tarts, biscuits and crackers are sure to make your mouth water.

They also serve one of Britain's best espresso's, the renowned Monmouth Coffee. There are a few small tables to enjoy your purchases and everything is naturally made, no artificial extras. Try walking past the window display without doubling back, seeking out your favourite bake and coming out with a paper bag filled with goodies.

ADDRESS

28A High Street
TR11 2AD

PHONE

07791 003183

NEAR HERE

Jam (p101)

The Chintz Symposium (p37)

Toro Studio (p122)

Did you know this guide is also available as an ebook?

The same great content but in a handy PDF
to keep on your phone, tablet or laptop.

Find out more at

bestofengland.com/ebooks

CHAPTER EIGHT

CULTURE

Museum of Witchcraft & Magic

CULTURE | BOSCASTLE | PL35 0HD

The Museum of Witchcraft and Magic is a museum dedicated to European witchcraft and magic and houses one of the world's largest collections of items relating to witchcraft and the occult. Since 1960, their collection has grown to more than 3,000 objects and some 7,000 books.

The museum was forced to move three times due to vandalism and pressure from the locals in the towns before settling here in its current home in the picturesque fishing port of Boscastle. In 2014, the museum came under the auspices of the Museum of British Folklore who added "Magic" to the museum's title.

ADDRESS
The Harbour
PL35 0HD

PHONE
01840 250111

NEAR HERE
Boscastle (p10)
Boscastle Farm Shop (p153)
The Mill House Inn (p48)

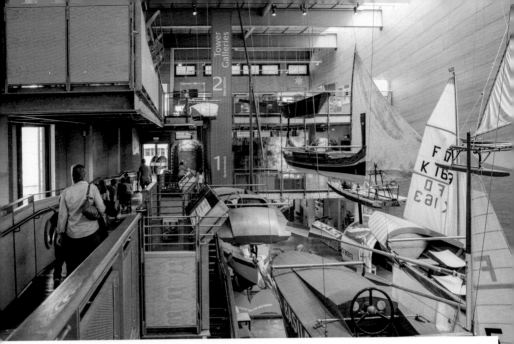

National Maritime Museum

CULTURE | FALMOUTH | TR11 3QY

Preserving Cornwall's maritime heritage is the National Maritime Museum located at Falmouth's Discovery Quay Harbour. The museum is an extensive attraction that provides an array of excellent exhibits bound to spark your interest.

Entering the museum you'll see an impressive collection of life size boats strung from the ceiling, alongside a smaller version of model boats, not forgetting the fascinating artefacts that have helped to form Cornwall's Maritime history. The museum is a great destination for kids as there is always something going on, from pirate puppet shows to mesmerising storytelling, which brings history to life.

ADDRESS
Discovery Quay
TR11 3QY

PHONE
01326 313388

NEAR HERE
Espressini Artisan Coffee (p104)
Cribbs Caribbean Cafe (p74)
Courtyard Deli & Kitchen (p109)

Penwith Gallery

CULTURE | ST. IVES | TR26 1NL

The Penwith Gallery and Society were founded and created in 1949 by a group of artists in St. Ives, including leading lights of the time such as Ben Nicholson, Barbara Hepworth and Bernard Leach. In 1960 a pilchard packing factory became the new gallery site and the gallery also acquired the building next door creating a truly interesting and dynamic space.

Natural light floods in from the open roofing and adds a depth of shadow to the many sculptures on display. Works from members and associates of the Society adorn the walls, and visitors can relax with a coffee from the café as they browse the artwork.

ADDRESS

Back Road West
TR26 1NL

PHONE

01736 795579

NEAR HERE

Fish Pye Pottery (p128)

Olives Cafe (p99)

Mount Zion Coffee (p98)

Porthminster Gallery

CULTURE | ST. IVES | TR26 2DY

Porthminster Gallery is a maze of interesting exhibition rooms displaying unique and vibrant artworks. This award-winning gallery is a bright, quayside gallery for British contemporary art located in a former warehouse by the sea in St. Ives.

This beautiful, deceptively large space represents more than fifty British Artists from up and coming locals to investment names. Modern and contemporary works by renowned artists can be found here as well as numerous diverse temporary exhibitions throughout the year. Porthminster Gallery is a must for those on the local art circuit.

ADDRESS
Westcotts Quay
TR26 2DY

PHONE
01736 795888

NEAR HERE
Armstrong & Wing (p133)
Scoff Troff Cafe (p108)
Alba Restaurant (p62)

Falmouth Art Gallery

CULTURE | FALMOUTH | TR11 2RT

The Falmouth Art Gallery is an impressive creative hub exhibiting works from major museum loans, local artists, community groups, school children and students. The exhibits rotate regularly, which makes for a dynamic and interesting display on every visit.

The collection ranges from Pre-Raphaelite and British Impressionist paintings to contemporary prints, photography and a children's illustration archive. The gallery has one of the largest collections of automata art, including fascinating and original moving sculptures and pieces made from wood and other media.

ADDRESS
Municipal Buildings
TR11 2RT

PHONE
01326 313863

NEAR HERE
The Falmouth Pottery (p123)
Cribbs Caribbean Cafe (p74)
Espressini Artisan Coffee (p104)

Circle Contemporary Gallery

CULTURE | WADEBRIDGE | PL27 7LR

The Circle Contemporary Gallery is part of the Hawksfield collective, a creative and dynamic hotspot for eating and shopping. The gallery showcases abstract and figurative works inspired by the natural landscape and includes pieces from home and abroad, along with fine collections of crafts, paintings and pottery.

The professional but relaxed gallery space is bright, cool and minimalist, and includes works by emerging and well-known artists, with the focus on fresh and innovative art. The collection is curated by Resident Artist John O'Carroll and Lucy Thorman, who carefully select work to impress visitors.

ADDRESS

Hawksfield
PL27 7LR

PHONE

01208 813220

NEAR HERE

The Arc Food Store (p141)

Strong Adolfos Cafe (p91)

Goose Shed (p120)

Royal Cornwall Museum

CULTURE | TRURO | TR1 2SJ

The Royal Cornwall Museum in Truro was set up 200 years ago to showcase historic objects and artefacts from Cornwall and around the world. Many of these archaeological items tell a story of Cornwall's past and inspire many visitors to learn about ancestry and art.

It is the only museum in Cornwall with permanent Ancient Greek, Roman and Egyptian displays, and a fine collection of rare ceramics. There are plenty of other exhibits too, including fine paintings, local history, rocks, fossils and gems. If nothing else, the world-famous collection of minerals, is sure to captivate you.

ADDRESS

25 River Street
TR1 2SJ

PHONE

01872 272205

NEAR HERE

Truro Arts Company (p132)

Falmouth Bay Cafe (p88)

Hubbox (p61)

Truro Cathedral

CULTURE | TRURO | TR1 2AF

Cornwall's only cathedral is a youngster as far as British cathedrals go and was built between 1880 and 1910. Designed by the leading Gothic Revival architect John Loughborough Pearson, this Cathedral is not just an amazing piece of architecture and place of worship, but also a concert hall and exhibitions space.

This was the first cathedral to be built on a new site in England since 1220 and due to the maritime climate, severe restoration was needed in 2002 after erosion of the stone. Beautiful stained glass and an impressive vaulted ceiling put Truro Cathedral up there with the most spectacular English cathedrals.

ADDRESS

14 St Mary's Street
TR1 2AF

PHONE

01872 276782

NEAR HERE

The Old Grammar School (p86)

Sam's in the City (p77)

Grounded (p103)

The Harbour Gallery

CULTURE | PORTSCATHO | TR2 5HF

The Harbour Gallery is located in the quiet coastal village of Portscatho. Evidence of the striking coastline is dramatically replicated on canvas in many of the artists' work, using oils, watercolours and other mediums.

The Gallery has a strong online presence with artists' podcasts and innovative ideas, also a wonderful zoom effect on their work shows minute details on paintings before considering a purchase. We think it's always best to view the art in person though and combined with a trip to Tatums for a coffee and a stroll on the beach, you have a great afternoon laid out.

ADDRESS

8A The Quay
TR2 5HF

PHONE

01872 580807

NEAR HERE

Tatams (p114)

Portscatho (p16)

The Watch House (p79)

Sandpiper Gallery

CULTURE | MOUSEHOLE | TR19 6QE

Run by Ben and Beccy Marshall, the Sandpiper gallery is an inviting space that exhibits beautiful paintings, pottery and glasswork. The gallery's interior has a Scandinavian feel, with bleached white flooring and walls that act as a neutral platform to display the works of art.

The attractive creations all have plenty of room, allowing the visitor an easy browsing experience and most of the items represent aspects of the Cornish coastline and local landscapes. This is a great gallery to find an unique piece of art to remember your visit to quaint Mousehole.

ADDRESS

2 Carn Topna
TR19 6QE

PHONE

01736 732441

NEAR HERE

The Rock Pool Cafe (102)

The Mousehole (p129)

2 Fore Street Restaurant (p51)

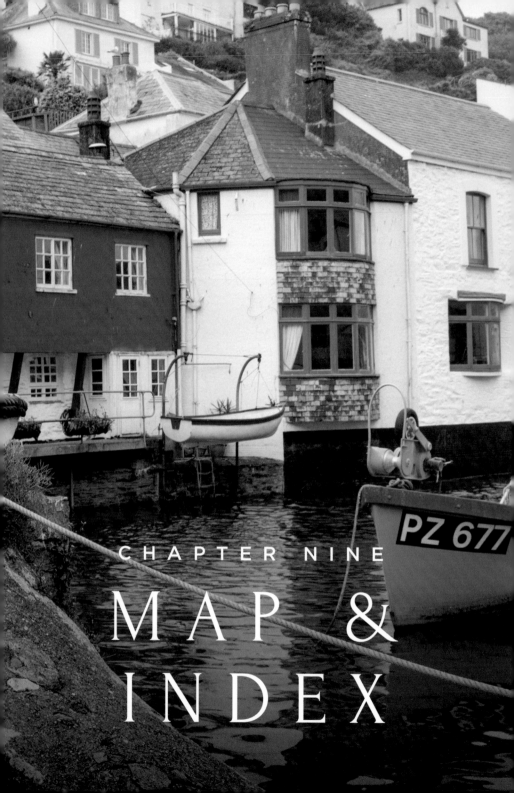

CHAPTER NINE

MAP &
INDEX

BEST OF ENGLAND

INSPIRING DISCOVERY

About Best of England

Honest Recommendations & Hidden Gems

What is Best of England?

Best of England is a curated
collection of travel
recommendations. Each one is
researched and has been visited
and photographed by a member of
the Best of England team.

Authenticity & integrity

None of the businesses in this travel
guide have paid to be included and we
visit every business that we
recommend. This guide is based on
our own experiences and opinions.
We think honesty is a really important
part of what we are trying to achieve.

Local knowledge is key

We believe there is nothing better
than local knowledge. That's why
we speak to the people that live
there to find out where to go.

Quality is everything

Quality is behind everything we do
and we will never compromise on
the recommendations we make.
We worry about the details from
the thickness of the paper to the
size of each font we use and we
hope that this effort is reflected in
the quality of our products.

Great content comes first

We use our photography to tell a story
for each of the businesses we
recommend. We want to bring each
one to life and inspire our readers to
visit themselves.

Tell us what you think

We are always on the look out for
ways to improve. Feedback is really
important to us in order to make the
best product possible. If you have
any suggestions or feedback then
please let us know via email to
info@bestofengland.com

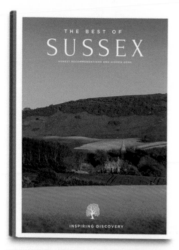

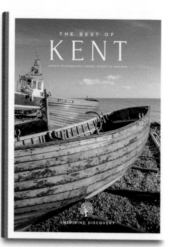

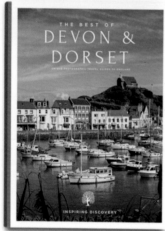

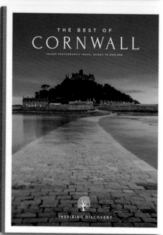

Meet the family

Honest Recommendations & Hidden Gems

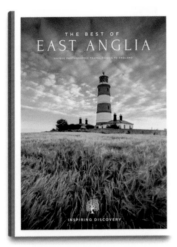

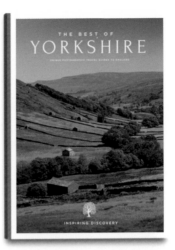

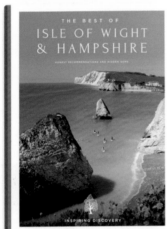

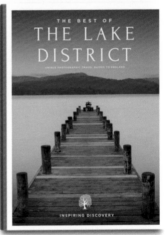

Enjoy 10% off your next purchase using the code: "bestoffriends"

www.bestofengland.com/books

Notes

Tried our app?

bestofengland.com/app

2 FORE STREET RESTAURANT	51	PORTHMINSTER KITCHEN	72
57 FORE STREET	73	PORTSCATHO	16
ALBA RESTAURANT	62	Q TEAROOM, STUDIO & GALLERY	105
ARMSTRONG & WING	133	QUAY BAKERY	156
BAKER TOM'S	118	RARE BITS	130
BEERWOLF BOOKS	33	READYMONEY COVE	14
BELLAMAMA DELI	142	RICK STEIN FISTRAL	66
BLACK DOG ANTIQUES & INTERIORS	131	RICK STEIN'S SEAFOOD RESTAURANT	71
BLUE TOMATO	111	ROCK BEACH	23
BLUEJEN FLORIST	135	ROCK POOL CAFÉ	102
BOSCASTLE	10	ROYAL CORNWALL MUSEUM	168
BOSCASTLE FARM SHOP	153	SAM'S IN THE CITY	77
BUDE SEA POOL	21	SANDPIPER GALLERY	171
BURGERS & FISH	63	SCOFF TROFF CAFE	108
BUTTERMILK	144	SHIP INN	44
CATCH SEAFOOD, BAR & GRILL	67	ST PETROC'S BISTRO	65
CIRCLE CONTEMPORARY GALLERY	167	STAR & GARTER	47
CORNISH MILL AND BAKEHOUSE	145	STEVENSON NEWLYN	143
COURTYARD DELI & KITCHEN	109	STONES BAKERY	157
CRIBBS CARIBBEAN CAFE & BAR	74	STRONG ADOLFO'S CAFÉ	91
DUCHY OF CORNWALL NURSERY	112	SUMMERLEAZE BEACH	27
EDEN PROJECT	12	SURF SHACK CAFÉ	96
ESPRESSINI ARTISAN COFFEE	104	TATUMS	114
FALMOUTH ART GALLERY	166	THE ALLOTMENT DELI	151
FALMOUTH BAY SEAFOOD CAFÉ	88	THE ARC SPECIALITY FOOD STORE	141
FALMOUTH POTTERY	123	THE BALCONY BAR & KITCHEN	60
FERRELL S H & SON	140	THE BEACH AT BUDE	81
FISH PYE POTTERY	128	THE BLUE PETER INN	36
FISTRAL BEACH	24	THE BOATHOUSE	89
FOWEY HARBOUR	17	THE CASTLE BUDE	13
GENKI CAFÉ	93	THE CHINTZ SYMPOSIUM	37
GOOSE SHED	120	THE CORNISH BARN	64
GROUNDED	103	THE DIGEY FOOD ROOMS	97
HALSETOWN INN	45	THE FRONT ROOM	110
HARBOUR FISH & CHIPS	59	THE GOLDEN LION	41
HAVENER'S	87	THE GRANARY	152
HEALEYS CORNISH CYDER FARM	146	THE GURNARD'S HEAD	32
HUB	75	THE HARBOUR FISH AND GRILL	70
HUBBOX	61	THE HARBOUR GALLERY	170
IAN LENTERN BUTCHERS	147	THE HONEY POT	100
IDLE ROCKS	56	THE KINGS ARMS	35
JAM	101	THE MILLHOUSE INN	48
JAMIE OLIVERS FIFTEEN	53	THE MOUSEHOLE	129
JOHNS WINE & SPIRIT SPECIALIST	124	THE MOWZER GALLERY	172
JUBILEE POOL	25	THE OLD GRAMMER SCHOOL	86
KILN	134	THE OLD QUAY HOUSE	58
LA BOCCA PIZZA KITCHEN	84	THE OLD SAIL LOFT	85
LOBBS FARM SHOP	150	THE SHARKSFIN	46
LOOE HARBOUR	15	THE SHIP INN	42
MACKEREL SKY SEAFOOD BAR	57	THE SORTING OFFICE	92
MEVAGISSEY	30	THE TINNERS ARMS	34
MINERS ARMS	43	THE WATCH HOUSE	79
MOUNT ZION COFFEE	98	THE WEBB STREET COMPANY	138
MUSEUM OF WITCHCRAFT & MAGIC	160	THREE PILCHARDS	40
NATIONAL MARITIME MUSEUM	161	TORO	122
NAUTILUS	121	TOWN & COUNTRY KITCHEN	113
NO. 56	125	TRAWLERS ON THE QUAY	78
OLD CUSTOM HOUSE	49	TREBARWITH STRAND	11
OLIVES CAFE	99	TRELAWNEY FISH	155
OUTLAW'S FISH KITCHEN	76	TRURO ARTS COMPANY	132
THE LOST GARDENS OF HELIGAN	26	TRURO CATHEDRAL	169
PENWITH GALLERY	162	YUMMEY SCRUMMY BAKERY	115
POLPERRO	20		
PORT GAVERNE HOTEL	80		
PORT ISAAC	22		
PORTHMINSTER CAFÉ	52		
PORTHMINSTER GALLERY	163		

Editor's Picks

1. Boscastle (p10)
2. The Lost Gardens of Heligan (p26)
3. The Gurnard's Head (p32)
4. Eden Project (p12)
5. 2 Fore Street Restaurant (p51)
6. Porthminster Cafe (p52)
7. Jamie Oliver's Fifteen (p53)
8. Idle Rocks (p56)
9. Alba Restaurant (p62)
10. Porthminster Gallery (p163)
11. Fowey Harbour (p17)
12. The Tinners Arms (p34)
13. Museum of Witchcraft and Magic (p160)
14. Healeys Cornish Cyder Farm (146)
15. Strong Adolfo's Cafe (p91)
16. Genki Cafe (p93)
17. Jubilee Pool (p25)
18. Polperro (p20)
19. The Old Quay House (p58)
20. National Maritime Museum (p161)

Padstow

15

Wadebridge

7

Newquay

16 **14**

2

Truro

A30

Redruth

20 **8**

10 **9**

12 **6**

3

St. Ives **A30**

17

5

Penzance **A394**

Helston

Land's End

Mousehole

Falmouth

Lizard